BALANCE IS BULL SHIT

Your Roadmap to a Thriving Marrriage,
Grounded Kids & Career Success

LORETTA SOFFE

BALANCE IS BULLSHIT
Your Roadmap to a Thriving Marriage, Grounded Kids & Career Success

© 2025 Loretta Soffe.

All rights reserved. No part of this publication may be reproduced, distributed, or transmitted in any form or by any means, including photocopying, recording, or other electronic or mechanical methods, without the prior written permission of the publisher, except in the case of brief quotations embodied in critical reviews and certain other noncommercial uses permitted by copyright law. For permission requests, please contact the author.

Independently Published by Loretta Soffe
  ISBN (Paperback): 979-8-9994932-1-7
  ISBN (Hardback): 979-8-9994932-2-4
  ISBN (EPUB): 979-8-9994932-0-0
Library of Congress Control Number (LCCN): 2025914582
Printed in the United States of America
Cover Design by Christian Rafetto, Humble Books
Manuscript Editing & Interior Layout by Wendy K. Walters

BALANCEISBULLSHIT.CO
LORETTASOFFE.COM

BALANCE IS **BULL SHIT**

DEDICATION

FOR DECLAN, HANK & ASHLEIGH—
Watching you grow into happy, kind, and curious humans has been the greatest joy of my life.

AND FOR SAM—
My best friend and partner in every sense of the word—thank you for building a life with me that we both love—and never settling for anything less.

BALANCE IS BULLSHIT

TABLE OF CONTENTS

1. THE TEXT THAT CHANGED EVERYTHING — 1
2. THE DEEP END — 15
3. MOVING DOWN THE PYRAMID—FROM CASHIER TO EVP — 29
4. WHEN IRISH EYES ARE SMILING — 43
5. THE COMPATIBILITY CODE — 57
6. TRADING PLACES — 77
7. THREE PREGNANCIES AND THREE PROMOTIONS — 89
8. BALANCING BABIES, BILLIONS, AND BOUNDARIES — 101
9. WHAT LOVE LOOKS LIKE — 119
10. STRONG DOESN'T MEAN INVINCIBLE — 141
11. SAM'S CASE FOR THE STAY-AT-HOME DAD — 155
12. A BOSS, A BITCH, OR A BOLD BRAVE LEADER? — 175
13. MENTORS MATTER — 201

14. OFF-RAMP TO ENTREPRENEURSHIP	221
15. OUR SECRET	235
16. RAISING FUTURE LEADERS	255
17. BUILDING OUR FAMILY CULTURE	275
18. PROOF OF CONCEPT	291
19. THE LIFE YOU CHOOSE	307
20. STORIES FROM SAM	315
21. THE NEXT CHAPTER IS YOURS	345

o n e

THE TEXT THAT CHANGED EVERYTHING

"Sometimes when things are falling apart, they may actually be falling into place."

UNKNOWN

GETTING FIRED

The stoplight at Sixth Avenue and Seneca was where my world started to crumble. One glance at my phone, one innocent-looking text from Pete Nordstrom, and twenty-five years of my life began dissolving in the space of a heartbeat.

"Hey Loretta, when you get into the office, swing by my desk."

Simple words. Devastating impact. My stomach dropped as my hands instinctively gripped the steering wheel tighter. This was not the message I wanted on my first day back from Christmas vacation.

I looked at my phone and said to myself, "... well, this is either going to be one of two things: It is either a welcome back or it's going to be the sweet goodbye."

I had returned from Cabo with a fresh tan and renewed energy, dressed for success in a short-sleeve V-neck Celine dress and Jimmy Choo booties. The outfit felt like armor now as I navigated the familiar path into Pacific Place parking garage, descending two and a half ramps to my usual executive spot. Everything about this morning followed our normal ritualistic routine—the same parking spot, the same walk to the elevator, the same path to the office. Except today, I skipped my regular stop at the outdoor espresso bar. My racing heart didn't need the caffeine.

For years, I believed in balance—like it was something I could earn if I just worked hard enough, planned well enough, cared more than most. I thought if I kept all the plates spinning, I'd find that sweet spot where career, marriage, and motherhood could peacefully coexist. But standing in that parking garage, heart pounding, I felt the truth wash over me: **balance is bullshit.** It's a myth we've been sold, and I was done buying it. What happened next would prove it—and change everything.

THE TEXT THAT CHANGED EVERYTHING

The sixth floor at Nordstrom's corporate headquarters housed the Nordstrom family and executive offices. As I walked down the familiar hallway, my assistant Jennifer's eyes told me everything I needed to know. The look she gave me spoke volumes—I was walking toward an execution, and we both knew it.

I took a deep breath as I entered Pete's office. It felt different that morning. The blinds were drawn, and they were never drawn. As he rose from his desk to join me at the corner table, his 6'5" frame seemed to loom larger than usual. The giant of retail was about to deliver a giant blow.

I walked in with butterflies in my stomach and my hands slightly shaking. With a little quiver in my voice, I stepped inside and said, "Hi, how's it going?"

He said matter-of-factly, "Why don't you have a seat right here."

I knew right then that this was going to be the conversation I had dreaded.

He took a moment to gather a few papers from his printer, and then he came over and sat down. I sat there quietly. My head was spinning. I said to myself, *Loretta, just stay calm and breathe. There's nothing you can't handle.*

As I finished saying those words to myself, he said, "Well, I've got something I want to talk to you about. This is not going to be easy. In fact, to be honest, this is one of the hardest conversations I've ever had to have."

I could feel his heartache and his sincerity. Pete is an upstanding person, honest and fair. We had a great relationship—both personally and professionally. My heart sank. I adjusted my legs and my back in the chair, straightening my shoulders as I prepared for the blow.

Pete continued, "Over the past couple of weeks, we've had some conversations with the board and amongst the executive team."

I nodded, and he continued, "You know the business has been tough, not what we wanted it to be, and the board made it clear they would no longer accept this kind of performance.

I realized right then exactly what he was saying - it's either you or me.

He paused, his voice carrying the weight of a decision already made. "I hate to say it, Loretta, but I need to take you out of your job."

"Pete! Everyone's business has been bad! At least ours is the best of the worst!" I burst out, barely letting him finish.

Rage boiled inside me as I sat in silence. After everything I'd done to turn things around—how could he do this?

"Loretta, I wish that mattered, but it doesn't," he sighed. "What matters is the board's expectations, and we haven't met them."

"Do you realize what we've been up against?" I countered. "The marketing team's failures, the contemporary department transition..." My mind raced as I defended my record of loyalty and dedication. "Had it not been for their mistakes, we would've made our numbers. This isn't fair!"

I was so mad. I felt so betrayed. I had given blood, sweat, and tears to this job and to the company for almost 25 years. I so badly wanted to debate his decision and try to prove him wrong.

He looked at me with genuine regret, but his response was firm: "I'm sorry, but the decision has been made."

I looked away from him, down at the table. In a split-second thought to myself, *I can either continue to challenge this, or I can take a deep breath and accept his decision with grace.*

"I get it," I said, "the ship has sailed."

He nodded.

"Do you have a plan in place for my replacement?" I asked.

"No," he shook his head, "We are going to do an external executive search. There is no one internally who is ready to take this on."

I responded, "I am happy to take a smaller role or stay on during the transition. This job is too big to have vacant. There are just too many daily decisions and too much at stake for the company."

"I don't think that is a good idea," he said," we will just have to make it work."

SLOW MOTION SHOCK

You know how in the movies, when a bullet is flying toward a soldier, and the scene switches to slow motion? Everything else blurs, and the shot rings out as the bullet spirals toward its mark. I had that surreal, slow-motion feeling as Pete ended the conversation—and, with it, my career.

With nothing more to say, I took the folder of papers in front of me, held back the tears, and tried to hold my head high as I walked out the door. Nearly 12 years of close collaboration, countless successes, and a strong professional rapport—all reduced to a three-minute conversation.

The walk from Pete's office felt surreal—as if I had a spotlight following me, certain everyone must know. Executive terminations were rare here.

Tears welled in my eyes as I approached my office. I felt hot. *Am I really fired?* I wondered. My assistant's desk was right outside my door. I took one look at her, and she just shook her head and said, "I'm really sorry."

For fear of completely breaking down, I just nodded, walked to my desk, and closed my door. I sat in my chair, collected my thoughts, and dialed Sam's number.

"Are you at home?" I said.

"Yeah," he answered, "Matt and Drew and the crew just got here to start the demo of the kitchen."

"Wow!" I sighed, "I forgot that was happening today. Well, I have some news."

THE TEXT THAT CHANGED EVERYTHING

"Yeah? What?" Sam inquired.

"Pete took me out of my job a few minutes ago …"

There was silence on the other end for a few seconds, and then Sam said, "I'm sorry, honey. Do you need me to come and get you?"

"No," I replied, fighting back tears. "I'm good. I'll just grab my bag and see you in a few minutes."

Jennifer sent out a notification to my team to meet in conference room 6K in 15 minutes. The irony wasn't lost on me; this room had hosted countless strategy sessions and celebrations. Now, it would be our last meeting.

They arrived quietly and promptly—the team who had worked tirelessly beside me to rebuild the business.

"Well," I began bravely, "my time here is over. We did our best, and I want each one of you to know how much I appreciate everything you have done. I believe in you. Keep working hard."

Through their muffled sniffles, I finished with, "I will miss all of you and will never forget all that we did together."

They got up out of their chairs and, one by one, left 6K in silence.

By 8:45 a.m., I was walking back to my car. In less time than it takes to watch a sitcom episode, everything I had known for over twenty-five years was gone. One text, one meeting, one conversation—that's all it took to end a career that had defined my life for a quarter of a century.

With that, I picked up my bag, grabbed my coat, gave Jennifer a bit of a nod, and walked down the hall into the elevator, out of the employee entrance, which would be the last time I would leave that entrance. I walked across the street and got back into my car.

"Am I dreaming, or did that actually just happen?" I said out loud, even though there was no one to hear me speak.

I drove home in a daze after scanning my garage pass. By the time I arrived, Sam had already told our builder and contractor about the news, even as they managed our kitchen demolition. They offered to leave, but I assured them to continue working. "I guess I'll be a little more involved now," I said.

Our kitchen was fully demolished by the end of the day. It was a metaphor for my career. Change was happening all around me.

> SOMETIMES, THE MOST SIGNIFICANT CHANGES IN OUR LIVES DON'T ARRIVE WITH WARNING BELLS AND SIRENS.

The Cabo tan suddenly felt like a cruel joke—a reminder of the vacation bliss that had preceded this professional apocalypse. As I drove away from Pacific Place that morning, I realized that sometimes, the most significant changes in our lives don't arrive with warning bells and sirens. They come in the form of a simple text message, waiting at a red light on what should have been just another Tuesday morning in Seattle.

BREAKING THE NEWS

It took a few days before I had the strength and courage to tell our kids. It was a few days later when we were in our RV up at the ski mountain we went to every weekend during the winter. This weekend was different because I wasn't racing to get home in time from either my office or the hangar from the private plane. This weekend, for the first time ever, I was home and able to help Sam prepare and load everything prior to the time the kids arrived off the bus from school.

Once we were settled at the mountain, Sam and I poured a glass of wine and said to the kids (who were 6, 8, and 10), "Guys, we have some exciting news to share with you!" Sam said.

"What?" they chorused.

"Mama is not going to be working at Nordstrom anymore," Sam delivered the message because I was still in shock and couldn't get the words out without crying.

Declan, who was 10, immediately asked, "What about your discount and your stock options?"

Wow, what astute questions, I thought.

"I don't get a discount anymore, Decca, but I get to keep my stock options."

Ashleigh, who was 6, asked, "Are you going to start playing tennis and paint your fingernails?" This was apparently the symbol for the moms in the neighborhood who stayed home with their kids.

I couldn't help but smile, "No, Ash, I'm not going to paint my nails or play tennis. But I will probably swim a bit more." *Hilarious*, I thought. I was always in desperate need of a manicure, and at just 6, Ashleigh apparently noticed!

"What about visiting you at your office? And going into that kitchen with all the candy?" Ash continued processing.

After a few moments of observing, Hank responded, "Guys, this is all we have ever wanted. Mama gets to be home with us!"

My tears still well up when I recall Hank's comment. For the first time in ten years of being a mom, I could finally prioritize being a mom before an executive. I was scared, but I was ready.

LESSONS LEARNED

When your world shifts without warning, remember:

- CHOOSE GRACE—Your response shapes both your legacy and your future opportunities. By choosing dignity over anger in Pete's office that morning, I preserved relationships and walked away without regrets. This conscious choice to exit with grace became a defining moment that I could look back on with pride rather than remorse.

THE TEXT THAT CHANGED EVERYTHING

- **IDENTITY BEYOND TITLE—**
  Your identity runs deeper than any corporate title or position. When my executive role was stripped away, I found my true foundation in being a mother and wife—roles that no termination could take away. This reminder helped me recognize that my worth wasn't tied to a company badge but to the enduring relationships that defined my life.

- **INTEGRITY IN EFFORT—**
  Your best effort matters, regardless of the outcome. Though my tenure ended differently than planned, I could walk away knowing I had given it my all—and that integrity let me hold my head high. When you pour yourself completely into your work, even unexpected endings can't diminish your sense of personal accomplishment.

- **EMBRACE CHANGE—**
  How you navigate crisis moments shapes your path forward. Instead of dwelling on the loss, I chose to focus on gratitude and what mattered most—my family. This shift in perspective transformed a professional ending into a personal beginning, opening doors I hadn't even known existed.

QUESTIONS FOR REFLECTION

1. Consider your current definition of success. How much of it is tied to your job title or position? What would remain if those external markers were stripped away?

   _____

   _____

   _____

2. Think about a moment when your professional identity was challenged or changed. What helped you maintain your core identity during that transition?

   _____

   _____

   _____

3. Recall a time when you had to choose between reacting with anger or grace. How did your choice impact the outcome and your relationships?

   _____

   _____

   _____

4. Think about your competing roles—professional, personal, family. If circumstances forced you to reprioritize them tomorrow, what would that look like?

_____

_____

_____

5. Remember a time when an ending became an unexpected beginning. What perspectives or relationships helped you navigate that transition?

_____

_____

_____

MY FAREWELL LETTER TO THE EMPLOYEES AT NORDSTROM

Dear All,

Many of you know that sports have played a very significant role in my life, both personally and professionally. Some of my clearest ideas have come to me while running or swimming. I just finished a long run on this beautiful, crisp January day. I've collected my thoughts and want to share them with you now.

The two words I have repeated too many times to count in the last week are that I am happy and grateful.

I'm eternally grateful for the incredible career that I've had at Nordstrom. For a company that promotes from within and keeps score every day, I'm grateful I won enough to keep moving down the pyramid over my 23 years. I'm grateful for all the experiences, challenges and relationships. I'm especially grateful for the 23-year education on merchandising, retailing, and serving people.

I'm really happy. Happy that I can spend some extra time playing with my kids and hanging out with my husband. I'm happy that I am starting a new and exciting chapter of our lives. I'm a firm believer in the saying, "the best is yet to come ..."

Most importantly, I'm happy that I can call the Nordstrom family my friends. Blake, Pete, Erik, Jamie—thank you for everything. I admire you all.

As my 9-year-old has said a number of times, "Don't worry, Mommy, there's always a happy ending." Yes, there is. It's already happy, and it's just the beginning.

Happy trails to all of you. Have fun. Keep winning.

BEST,
LORETTA

t w o

THE DEEP END

"The beginning of life writes its story on us; the rest of life is ours to write."

ANONYMOUS

HOW DISCIPLINE BUILT INDEPENDENCE

I was five the first time I jumped into the deep end—alone, unprompted, and fearless. While other kids clung to the wall in the shallow end, I already knew the best things in life happen where your feet can't touch.

Each morning during the summer months, I'd make my own way to the pool—crossing the street, cutting through the trees, and marching onto the deck where my older siblings practiced. Without hesitation, I'd head straight for the diving board and plunge in before anyone could stop me—much to my mother's horror. That same spirit had me racing up the center aisle of St. Monica's Catholic Church during Sunday mass at age two, my Linus-sized blanket trailing behind me as I announced, "N-o-o-o-o, I wanna see Holy God!" My mother's gentle Irish lilt would echo through the church: "Oh Loretta, come back!"

Coming back wasn't really my style, even then. Being the youngest of five in a first-generation Irish immigrant family meant I was always diving into the deep end—whether it was up church aisles, across our street to the swimming pool, or toward my own version of the American Dream my parents had chosen. They'd taken their own plunge into the unknown when they left Ireland for my dad to accept an engineering job at Boeing in Seattle. They crossed the Atlantic with four children, me on the way, and just five suitcases.

That leap of faith landed us on Mercer Island, where my parents bought a home for the seven of us, across from a swim and tennis club—a place that would shape my destiny in ways none of us could have imagined. Our little island, where my husband and I live today, is surrounded by Lake Washington and connected west to Seattle and east to Bellevue (the two main cities nearby) by two bridges. Mercer Island became our own piece of paradise: just seven miles long and thirteen miles around, home to 25,000 people, with three grocery stores, one high school, and the Catholic church that anchored our family's life.

THE DEEP END

THE DEEP WATERS OF DISCIPLINE

With determination and a shoestring budget, my parents transformed an empty house into our home—one careful purchase at a time. It was just the necessities: beds, tables, and the thick tapestry curtains my mom had brought in one of our five suitcases. Our living room coffee table displayed the parting gifts my dad had received when they left Ireland—model airplanes, handcrafted monkey wood bowls, and other traditional Irish treasures. While my friends' homes boasted "bonus rooms" with plush sectional couches and big color TVs, we had an unfinished basement and a single black-and-white TV with just three channels.

Eventually, we got a ping pong table that became the center of endless tournaments with neighborhood kids. We made the most of our free time, transforming our unfinished basement into anything we could dream up—a pretend school, a travel agency selling trips to exotic places like Ireland, and sometimes even a disco where we'd blast our favorite 70s music. Earth, Wind & Fire, The Jackson 5, and Neil Diamond were on regular rotation. Under the stairs, we created a secret fort, lining the floor with thick sleeping bags and mounding our pillows into the walls. In the summer months, we practically lived at the swim club across the street, turning picnic tables into fortresses with towels and blankets. With white zinc oxide smeared down our noses, we looked like a pack of little raccoons—wild and free.

Like a one-woman pit crew, my mom kept our split-level home spotless—mopping floors, dusting furniture, and making sure we understood that cleanliness was more than just tidiness; it was about respect and discipline. Every corner of our home reflected her belief that how we cared for what little we had mattered more than having plenty. What felt like scarcity at the time—our modest home with a single TV and an unfinished basement—turned out to be my parents' greatest investment. They taught us that strength doesn't come from abundance. It comes from making the most of what you have, and from the pride that grows when nothing is wasted.

> EVERY CORNER OF OUR HOME REFLECTED MY MOTHER'S BELIEF THAT HOW WE CARED FOR WHAT LITTLE WE HAD MATTERED MORE THAN HAVING PLENTY.

Our home ran like a well-oiled Irish machine—part convent, part boot camp. Each morning began with the same rituals: my mom moving from room to room with China teacups filled with hot tea, drawing open our blinds singing "It's a beautiful day!"—rain or shine. Then came the familiar current of our days: morning mass, school, sports, homework, and only then, if we'd earned it, play.

Being the youngest of five by several years meant I experienced our family differently from my siblings. My brother, twelve years my senior, and my three sisters, all born within four years of each other, all treated me as their favorite. We played together endlessly, swam on the swim team together, played tennis together, and turned endless games of hide and seek into epic adventures throughout our house. I loved having four siblings—it was like our own little tribe. There was a special benefit to being the youngest, though I didn't always appreciate it at the time: having multiple parent figures, especially my brother, who managed his four younger sisters with patience beyond his years. He'd often say I gave him "a run for his money," particularly when it came to my more than picky eating habits. I tested his patience every chance I got, but he never gave up on me.

A HOUSE OF FAITH

Our family life centered in the Catholic faith, which meant more than just Sunday Mass—it was an integral part of every day. Each morning before school at St. Monica, my mom would have all 5 of us seated in a pew for 8 a.m. mass, not mandatory but essential in her mind, and at 8:30, we would find our friends and make our way to our classrooms. Weekends always included at least one church service, Saturday at 5 p.m. or Sunday morning. After mass on Sundays, we would change out of our "Sunday best" and gather in our small kitchen to make lunch. My dad was a stranger in the kitchen except on Sunday mornings when his ritual was frying the bacon (still rashers to him) with tomatoes. While other families were flipping pancakes or making waffles, we held onto our Irish breakfast traditions—thick-cut bacon, eggs, and warm soda bread slathered with butter and orange marmalade. The sounds of those mornings are forever etched in my memory: rashers crackling in Dad's favorite cast iron pan, the whistling tea kettle, and Dad singing old Irish tunes.

Sundays were sacred in our house, not just because of Mass but because of these simple rituals that bound us together. My love of Sundays has stayed with me since those childhood days. While my friends dreaded Sunday nights, I never got the blues anticipating the week ahead—my parents had taught us to see Sunday as a day of rest and celebration, not a day to dread. Looking back, I realize how their quiet wisdom about savoring these days shaped not just our weekends, but our outlook on life's natural rhythms.

EARLY MORNING WATERS

By age six, I was breaking swimming records in the eight-and-under age group. I became such a fixture at the pool that I became the team mascot, and the team's rallying cry became "Get back, Loretta," inspired by a famous Beatles' song.

As I entered seventh grade and my swimming commitment grew, my coach suggested I add twice-daily practices. Without hesitation, my mom supported me. Our 4:45 a.m. alarms marked the beginning of daily expeditions into the deep end of discipline. Bundled against the pre-dawn chill, my mom would drive through darkness to the pool in our 1969 Ford LTD station wagon with its broken heater. While other parents dozed in their cars after dropping their kids off, my mom would lace up her running shoes and navigate her own challenging waters, jogging six miles in the cold and dark streets nearby. After practice, we would share breakfast at Denny's before Mass and school. Looking back, I realize these early morning rituals taught me more than just discipline—they showed me what it means to support someone's dreams, no matter the personal cost. I still carry that lesson with me: find the time, make the time, and move your body—even if it means a freezing 5 a.m. swim or a jog in the dark. (More on that later.)

For as long as I can remember, before my races, my mom would pray with me: "God give me the strength, courage, and endurance to do my best (and to win)." That prayer, which I have since shared with my own kids, became more than just words before a race—it was a compass for navigating life's deeper waters. The courage to step up to the starting blocks, the endurance to push through the 1500-meter freestyle, a grueling 15-minute race—these lessons transcended the pool and became tools for facing challenges in coaching, business leadership, and parenthood. These dawn immersions were teaching me that success in deep waters requires both faith and fortitude.

SWIMMING AGAINST THE CURRENT

The independence I'd developed through swimming was about to extend beyond the pool. My parents made it very clear that all of us would go to Catholic schools, no questions asked. All four of my siblings had dutifully followed this family mandate, attending Catholic school from kindergarten through high school—there was never any discussion of alternatives. But after two years at a private Jesuit high school twenty-five minutes from home, I made my own decision. Without asking my parents for permission, I dove into unknown waters, leaving my private Catholic school for public education. At age 16, I left the house on a summer morning with a good friend and headed to registration day at the local public high school. I returned thirty minutes later, simply showing my mom my class schedule for Mercer Island High School. There was no fight. No grounding. Just a long look from my mom that said she knew I was no longer asking for permission—I was charting my own course. The first day as a junior at a new school felt like swimming in open water - no lane lines, no familiar faces. But those years of early morning practices had taught me how to navigate unfamiliar currents.

THE DEEPEST DIVE

College recruitment became my first true deep-water solo swim. While my peers had their parents testing the waters for them, I navigated the depths alone. When I was being recruited for college swimming, I visited schools across the country alone, negotiating my scholarship and, ultimately, choosing Berkeley. While my friends' parents were busy preparing their kids for college, I packed up my life and shipped my boxes before traveling with my coach and teammates to a swim meet in Florida and then to the Olympic trials. Three weeks later, when I arrived in Berkeley, I found my labeled boxes stacked in the university gym, and I moved myself into my freshman dorm. My parents did not help with move-in—in fact, they did not come for a swim meet or visit campus until graduation. It was not their custom to travel unnecessarily; this was an extra expense they could not afford. Fortunately, I found a best friend in Jill, whose parents became my surrogate family and support system. But regardless, day in and day out, every challenge, triumph, and setback became my solo journey to navigate.

DAY IN AND DAY OUT, EVERY CHALLENGE, TRIUMPH, AND SETBACK BECAME MY SOLO JOURNEY TO NAVIGATE.

I had officially learned to swim in open water—without a lifeguard, without instructions, and without a fallback plan.

FINDING MY LANE

Looking back, I realize that the most precious gifts often come wrapped in challenge. From my parents' brave leap across the Atlantic to my mother's pre-dawn runs while I swam, our family's story was written in small acts of courage. The discipline I learned in those morning practices, diving into the dark pool before sunrise, mirrored the grit my parents showed in building our American life. Like the Irish seas they crossed, each challenge taught me to move forward even when I couldn't see the shore.

That little girl running up the church aisle never did learn to "come back"—she only learned to dive deeper: into water, into work, into whatever came next. Whether into pre-dawn practices, new schools, or life a thousand miles from home, I didn't wait at the edge. My parents' structure hadn't kept me in the shallow end; it had taught me to swim in any depth. Discipline wasn't a constraint—it was my superpower. From my parents' example, I learned that success isn't about waiting for perfect conditions; it's about diving into the deep end, even when you can't see the bottom.

LESSONS LEARNED

- **RESILIENCE IS EARNED—**
  Every 5 a.m. practice taught me that resilience is built one cold plunge at a time. When you consistently prove to yourself that you can do hard things, you develop the mental toughness to face any challenge. The secret? Embrace the discomfort; don't avoid it.

- **SACRIFICE IS WORTH IT—**
  Things worth doing are worth the price of doing them. The sacrifices my parents made for our family paved the way for my siblings and me to step into possibilities we could never have imagined had they remained in Ireland.

- **DISCIPLINE DRIVES PROGRESS—**
  My mother taught me discipline before I knew its name—running six miles in the dark while I swam, keeping our home immaculate, and turning daily routines into rituals. I carry her example in all that I do: show up, do the work, and trust that small, consistent efforts lead to lasting success.

- **FAITH ANCHORS US—**
  Faith isn't just about church pews and Sunday Mass. It's about having a foundation solid enough to support you when you're diving into life's deep ends. Whatever form your

faith takes, finding your True North serves as a compass for life's boldest leaps.

QUESTIONS FOR REFLECTION

1. Think about a time when you had to push through something difficult. What gave you the strength to persevere? Like those early morning practices, what did that experience teach you about your own resilience?

   _____

   _____

   _____

2. Who has made quiet sacrifices for your success—perhaps in ways you didn't recognize at the time? Like my mother's pre-dawn runs, how have others supported your dreams through their own parallel journeys?

   _____

   _____

   _____

3. What traditions or values from your upbringing seemed limiting at the time but have proven to be gifts? How has "making do with less" shaped your approach to success?

_____

_____

_____

4. Which daily disciplines in your life right now are moving you toward your goals? What consistent habits are you building that will create your foundation for success?

_____

_____

_____

5. When have you chosen the harder path, like switching schools or moving away, because you knew it was right for you? What gave you the courage to make that leap?

_____

_____

_____

THAT LITTLE GIRL RUNNING UP THE CHURCH AISLE NEVER DID LEARN TO "COME BACK"—SHE ONLY LEARNED TO DIVE DEEPER: INTO WATER, INTO WORK, INTO WHATEVER CAME NEXT.

three

MOVING DOWN THE PYRAMID— FROM CASHIER TO EVP

"Surround yourself with good people, honor them, trust them, and expect the most from them—and you will be successful."

BRUCE NORDSTROM

EARLY INFLUENCES

I never planned to build a career in fashion. In fact, when my sister called me from her Nordstrom office asking for advice on color combinations and stripe patterns, I couldn't help but laugh.

I was living in my sorority house at UC Berkeley, answering calls on one of the two landlines mounted in the vestibule. Annette, my older sister and a regional buyer at Nordstrom, would ask what colors I thought would sell better.

"Annette," I'd roll my eyes, wedging the phone between my ear and my shoulder, "I'm at Cal. I'm buying blue and gold, not red. (God forbid—Stanford's color!) I have no clue what customers want."

But everything changed one weekend when I stayed with her.

Annette spent most of our time spread out at her dining table, studying line sheets and building her buy for the next season. I watched ... and before I realized it, I got pulled in.

Retail wasn't just about picking cute clothes—it was a fascinating blend of creativity and analysis. Color palettes, prints, and patterns told a story. But behind all the beauty were pricing strategies, forecasting models, margin calculations, and customer behavior trends.

Somewhere between the colors and the calculations, a seed was planted—one I didn't even realize was there yet.

STARTING FROM THE BOTTOM

After graduation from Cal in 1988, reality hit hard.

My dad made it crystal clear: I was officially off the payroll. If I wanted to stay in the Bay Area, I had to figure it out myself.

Armed with a business and economics degree—but no experience, no mentors, and not much of a network—I dreamed of working in sports marketing. But the job market didn't care about my dreams. Interviews came and went. So did my first-choice jobs.

I thought about studying for the LSAT or GMAT, but I didn't have the luxury of not working. Necessity became the mother of invention. I needed a place to live... and a job. Fast.

Annette offered me the storage room in her apartment (yes, a literal storage room) and encouraged me to take a temporary cashier job during the big Nordstrom Anniversary Sale. With a leap of faith, I hopped into her car for my first day. She handed me an employee number and a quick tutorial on how to ring sales. No formal training—just a crash course and a smile. I have no idea how many mistakes I made that first day, but that's how it all began.

At the time, I thought it was just a placeholder—a way to make ends meet until I found a "real" job. But that summer job changed everything.

HUMBLING BEGINNINGS

Working retail while my friends were launching high-profile careers in finance and advertising was humbling, to say the least.

It felt like everyone I knew was speeding ahead—new jobs, new apartments, new cars—while I was folding sweaters and ringing sales in a mall.

There were moments when I couldn't help but wonder if I had taken a wrong turn somewhere.

But two weeks later, I got my first paycheck.

Six weeks after that, I had enough saved to move into a real apartment with my friend Jill.

It wasn't glamorous, but it was progress—and progress felt good.

Growing up, my parents had drilled into me the values of hard work, grit, and personal accountability. Swimming had taught me to stay focused on my own lane, no matter how fast or flashy the swimmers around me seemed. That mindset became invaluable. Instead of spiraling into doubt or jealousy, I poured my energy into the job right in front of me. I set daily sales goals. I stayed late to unpack new merchandise. I learned my customers' names and their preferences. It wasn't the career I had imagined. But it was a start. And more importantly, it was mine.

> INSTEAD OF SPIRALING INTO DOUBT OR JEALOUSY, I POURED MY ENERGY INTO THE JOB RIGHT IN FRONT OF ME

THE INVERTED PYRAMID

At Nordstrom, there's an "inverted pyramid" philosophy: The customer sits at the top, and the executive team sits at the very bottom, serving everyone above them. Promotion didn't mean climbing higher. It meant moving "lower"—getting even closer to the people and customers who drove the business. I absolutely thrived in that environment.

My results steadily paid off. I moved from cashier to sales associate. From sales associate to department manager. And after almost ten rejections (yes, ten!), I finally earned a coveted role as a regional buyer based in San Francisco. Now, I was managing a $50 million annual P&L across ten Northern California stores. At 24 years old, with no hair dryer, no blazer, and no idea what I was doing—I was officially a buyer.

GRIT, GROWTH, AND GUT INSTINCTS

Life finally felt on track. Being a buyer was like being an entrepreneur—but even better.

I had creative freedom backed by the security of a big company. I vividly remember sitting in a regional meeting in San Francisco when a Nordstrom family member asked, "Who's going to lead this company someday?" Without hesitation, I raised my hand.

BALANCE IS BULLSHIT

I was 28 years old. I didn't have a five-year plan. But I had the gut instinct and the confidence to believe I could do it, no matter what it took. Looking back, I'm amazed at my boldness. But that's who I was.

The path wasn't always smooth. While I was grinding away, one of my friends was hopping from job to job every two years, doubling her salary each time. I couldn't help but wonder if I was missing out. My boyfriend at the time dismissed my career in retail as "cute"—a comment that left me doubting myself more than I cared to admit.

Meanwhile, I was still swimming competitively—open water races, triathlons—most of which were held on Saturdays, sacred workdays in retail. Staying in shape meant swimming three nights a week at a pool forty minutes away from work. It meant asking for Saturdays off for races and negotiating early leaves to make practice. It meant advocating for myself in ways that didn't come naturally back then.

I wrestled with these competing demands daily.

Should I quit?

Should I pivot?

Was I playing too small?

The internal complaints started stacking up—until one day, I realized they weren't serving me at all. Instead of worrying if I made the right decision, I decided to make the decision right. I was doing good work. I was making good money. I was building a real career. No, it wasn't perfect. Yes, sometimes I worked until 8 p.m. and ate dinner standing over the sink.

But I could run in the mornings. I could swim at night. And I wasn't stuck behind a desk feeling unfulfilled. So, I stayed the course. And that decision changed everything.

HOMECOMING

In 1995, I moved back to Seattle to take a role in Nordstrom's Product Development Division. Life fell into place. I reconnected with Sam—a high school friend who would later become my husband—and felt a deep sense of coming home. The job itself was tough. Honestly, I hated it. There were days I seriously considered packing it all up and moving back to San Francisco. But a few key mentors convinced me to stick it out. I learned lessons that would stay with me for the rest of my career—how to analyze the cost of goods, manage margins, and navigate technical design and fit. More importantly, I learned how to thrive even when the work didn't feel exciting. That season taught me that passion doesn't always come first. Sometimes, perseverance has to lead the way.

BREAKTHROUGHS

In 1997, I got a call: A buyer was going out on maternity leave, and they needed someone to fill in. I jumped at the opportunity, and performed so well that they offered me the job full-time. It became one of my favorite roles: National Buyer for Women's Contemporary Design Apparel (the Savvy department, for old-school Nordstrom shoppers), managing a $75 million P&L. I won numerous awards during that time. But more importantly, I learned a critical truth: Performance is your best resume. My results caught the attention of the Nordstrom family—and my career trajectory shifted overnight.

CLIMBING (OR RATHER, MOVING LOWER)

Between 1998 and 1999, my consistent recognition led to a major promotion. Pete Nordstrom promoted me to Vice President, General Merchandise Manager for Juniors—and later, Contemporary Apparel. My P&L responsibility exploded from $75 million to $250 million—and then $500 million by 2001. At 32, I became the youngest Vice President in company history.

To be totally honest, at first, I felt completely in over my head and had a touch of imposter syndrome. But I discovered the secret: It wasn't about having all the answers. It was about being humble enough to listen, curious enough to learn, and brave enough to try my best anyway. I shared the lessons I had learned as a buyer, teaching my team how to spot opportunities, analyze data, and drive performance.

Despite the steep learning curve, I consistently delivered results. Four years later, in 2005, I was promoted again—this time to Executive Vice President, General Merchandise Manager for all of Women's Wear. I was the youngest EVP (who wasn't a Nordstrom) in company history.

THE BIG LEAGUES

The EVP role was three times the size of my previous job, and the biggest responsibility held by a non-family member. I was leading a $1.5 billion business with three kids under four years old at home. (Yes, you read that right.)

The division, the largest in the company, had been underperforming for decades. Turning it around wasn't optional, which would require a total transformation of both strategy and organizational structure. It meant making tough decisions, including letting go of three vice presidents—peers who were ten years my senior, one of whom had even hired me as a buyer.

But I knew if you manage mediocrity, that's exactly what you get. If I were going to succeed, I had to surround myself with winners.

I hired Boston Consulting Group to do a deep dive into the customer base, the competitive landscape, and the market. Over 6-9 months, we developed a comprehensive strategy that put the customer at the center of everything we did.

The results were transformative: We grew the business from $1.5 billion to $2.0 billion in four years. We increased profit by $90 million. We built new categories, created extraordinary brand partnerships, accelerated e-commerce growth, and redefined what a customer-centric assortment strategy meant at scale.

LIFE IN THE BOARDROOM

As EVP, I had a regular seat in the boardroom—and with it, a front-row seat to both the highs and the brutal realities of running a public company. Wall Street analysts requested one-on-one meetings with me to understand our strategy. Women's Wear Daily named me a "Rising Star." My peers voted me MVP multiple times.

But every quarterly meeting felt like waterboarding. The scrutiny was relentless. The pressure was constant. Thank God for my swimming and yoga background—without knowing how to breathe deeply and stay calm, I'm not sure I would have survived it.

There were incredible highs—private planes, front row seats at runway shows in New York, London, and Paris, meeting people like Oprah, Anna Wintour, Justin Timberlake, and Bono. But the lows were just as real—the constant stress, the fear of missing targets, and the never ending demands from shareholders, board members, and the Nordstrom family.

It was the ride of a lifetime.

Besides, from that accidental summer job as a cashier, I made my way to the boardroom as EVP—and I wouldn't change a thing. The lessons Nordstrom taught me—about service, respect, humility, and leadership—didn't just shape my career. They shaped who I became.

LESSONS LEARNED

- **EMBRACE IMPERFECTION—**
  I was never truly "ready" for any of the jobs I had. Instead of waiting until I felt fully prepared, I learned to trust my instincts, ask questions, and dive in. You don't need to have it all figured out—fake it until you make it.

- **REDEFINE SUCCESS—**
  Success isn't about following a preset path or chasing a specific title. It's about discovering your strengths, digging deep, and excelling where you are right now.

- **RESULTS MATTER—**
  Performance is your best resume. The path won't always be straight, but what matters most are the lessons learned along the way—and the consistent results you deliver.

- **EMPOWER OTHERS—**
  Your success as a leader depends on empowering your team. It's not about having all the answers—it's about building trust, fostering ownership, and teaching others how to spot opportunities. That's how you create extraordinary results.

QUESTIONS FOR REFLECTION

1. When have you stepped into something before you felt fully ready? How did it change you?

   _____

   _____

   _____

2. What holds you back from saying yes to roles or challenges that stretch you?

   _____

   _____

   _____

3. What non-negotiable values guide your career decisions today?

   _____

   _____

   _____

MOVING DOWN THE PYRAMID—FROM CASHIER TO EVP

4. How do you define and measure success in your current role, beyond just titles or paychecks?

   _____

   _____

   _____

5. What daily actions are you taking to build your track record of results and impact?

   _____

   _____

   _____

HARD WORK, GRIT, AND PERSONAL ACCOUNTABILITY—THIS WAS THE INVALUABLE MINDSET THAT LED TO MY SUCCESS.

f o u r

WHEN IRISH EYES ARE SMILING

> *"May the road rise to meet you. May the wind be always at your back. May the sun shine warm upon your face, the rains fall soft upon your fields, and until we meet again, may God hold you in the palm of His hand."*
>
> IRISH BLESSING

I'm writing this on the one-year anniversary of Mom's death, tears mixing with my morning coffee as I sit in the quiet darkness before dawn—her time of day. As she lived her life—with quiet faith and gentle grace—she slipped away in her sleep after giving her caregiver a smile, a nod, and a whispered thank you. I can almost see her spirit rising straight up to heaven, reunited with Dad, my brother Colin, my nephew Ryan, and all those who went before. She was the last of her generation, closing a chapter written in faith, love, and that stubborn Irish devotion I've come to cherish.

They say you're a blend of those who raised you—their strengths and weaknesses flowing through your veins. In my case, these waters run deep and true. From my mother, I inherited her grit, discipline, structure, and everlasting optimism. Her meticulous habits became the framework upon which I built my life. From my father, I learned the value of hard work and sacrifice coupled with his free spirit, spontaneity, and an ability to find humor and laughter in just about every situation. From both, I got the gift of love, sacrifice, and, most importantly, faith. Together, they created not just a home but a foundation. My mother's quiet determination and my father's infectious charm weren't contradictions but complementary forces, teaching me that balance isn't found in choosing one path but in learning to dance between them.

As I reflect on the differences between my mom and dad, I see how perfectly they balanced our family—like the sunrise and sunset blessing each day.

MY MOTHER—
DISCIPLINE AND GRACE

My mom ran our house like a tight ship. I can still hear the dishwasher running at 9:00 p.m. every night as she went about her evening routine—turning off lights, locking doors, and shutting the house down for the day. Long before we stirred, she would start her day in the dark with her Bible and hot tea, wrapping each of us in her morning prayers before beginning her carefully orchestrated routine. Room by room, she'd wake us with a steaming cup of tea, opening our blinds while singing, "Isn't it a beautiful day?"—even under Seattle's cloudiest skies.

Every detail was managed with care and purpose. Our days began with 8 a.m. morning Mass before the 830 a.m. school start, where she'd have us all dressed in school uniforms, standing in the pew like little soldiers. After school, she'd be waiting with healthy snacks laid out on the kitchen counter—apple slices, carrot sticks, and her famous peanut butter celery boats. Then came the afternoon parade of carpools to practices, all while somehow preparing dinner for seven of us. After we'd eaten, she'd take her familiar spot at the dinner table to make the next day's lunches: five sandwiches, five treats, five pieces of fruit, and, yes, more celery with peanut butter. Never frazzled, just methodically organized. These daily rituals weren't just about keeping order—they were her way of showing up for us, day after day, with consistency, discipline, and love.

THESE DAILY RITUALS WEREN'T JUST ABOUT KEEPING ORDER—THEY WERE HER WAY OF SHOWING UP FOR US, DAY AFTER DAY

BALANCE IS BULLSHIT

The Catholic church on Mercer Island, St. Monica, became her sanctuary, where she found both her community, solace, and purpose. One of her many volunteer duties was leading the rosary on Saturdays before the 5 p.m. Mass. What started as just a few joining her transformed into nearly ten pews of parishioners, drawn by her quiet holiness and soft voice. Her humble grace and gentle spirit created a presence others sought out. Over the years, I'd often hear people whisper, "She's like a saint among us,"—and watching her there, I knew they were right.

Her determination showed in unexpected ways. You could set your watch by her routines until the very end. On Monday, Wednesday, and Friday, after daily morning Mass, she'd run six miles down Island Crest Way on Mercer Island. Tuesdays, Thursdays, and Saturdays found her swimming a mile at our swim club. She became a beloved fixture in the local running circuit, consistently ranking first or second in her age group. She'd come home with this mischievous glint in her eye, laughing as she described racing someone twenty years her junior across a finish line to improve her time. This level of determination and resolve is not surprising when you learn that my mom took a vow with a friend when they were 14 years old never to drink alcohol—and she never did.

At 60, when most people settle into comfortable retirement, she tackled her first marathon. I can still see her layering up for those training runs through dark Seattle winters, undaunted by rain, cold, or darkness. Now, when I force myself out for a dog walk in the rain or brave a winter plunge in the lake, I smile, knowing exactly where my grit comes from. I got her grit, but I love tequila too much to completely swear off alcohol!

One of my favorite memories of her captures her thoughtful nature perfectly: On cold winter evenings, she would surprise the lifeguards at the swim club with steaming bowls of tomato soup and perfectly grilled cheese sandwiches. She'd carefully prepare everything extra hot, then carefully balance the trays with their meals and deliver it to them in the bubble where they watched over the swimmers. They never asked for this kindness—she simply noticed their long shifts in the chilly air and decided they needed warming from the inside out.

This quiet generosity defined her. Much to our teenage mortification, Mom would often stop for hitchhikers along Island Crest Way. When we'd protest, she'd simply say, "I hate to see them stranded there." She never turned away anyone who knocked on our door looking for odd jobs, either. Whether it was raking leaves or washing windows, she'd find work for them, determined to help anyone in any way possible.

MY FATHER—
WARMTH AND SACRIFICE

When I was little, my dad was like a real-life leprechaun to me. His Irish accent colored every story about childhood adventures and pranks played on siblings and friends—he would barely get through telling them before melting into hysterical laughter. He loved people and parties, and when he could not be on the golf course or at the horse track, you would find him watching whatever sport was playing on TV. Those hours we spent together watching games became some of my earliest and fondest memories with him.

He provided the perfect counterbalance to my mother's disciplined nature—relaxed and jovial, considering a round of golf plenty of exercise for any day. Though he'd been a scratch golfer back in Ireland, he set aside his clubs during our busy childhood years when our activities demanded weekend attention. It was just one of countless quiet sacrifices he made for our family.

One of my favorite childhood memories captures his playful spirit perfectly. Just as my mom would be preparing one of her famously healthy dinners, he'd catch my eye with a mischievous grin and whisper, "Hey Roo"—my nickname since I was tiny—"how about we sneak down to Dairy Queen for an ice cream cone?" My answer was always an enthusiastic "Sure, let's do it!" These small adventures with him were like stolen moments of pure joy, made sweeter by their spontaneity.

A FATHER'S SILENT STRENGTH

I feel I was the lucky one among my siblings, gifted with countless hours of one-on-one time with my dad during our swim meet travels. Those long drives and hotel stays became our special time together, revealing layers of my father I might never have known otherwise. Unlike the pressure-driven swim parents surrounding us, Dad was my unwavering cheerleader. His response never varied—a warm "Great job!" followed by the inevitable "How about McDonald's?"—whether I'd won or missed the wall completely.

These trips showed me a side of him others rarely saw. Each night in our hotel rooms, I'd watch him quietly kneel beside his bed to pray. There was something profound in seeing your dad, a small Irishman, in such private moments of devotion—a lesson in faith more powerful than any sermon I'd heard.

Only years later did I fully grasp the weight he carried. He'd pick me up from evening practices at 7:30 p.m., somehow still smiling after his marathon workday. When I entered the corporate world, struggling to stay past 6 p.m., the magnitude of his dedication finally hit me. This was a man

> THERE WAS SOMETHING PROFOUND IN SEEING YOUR DAD, A SMALL IRISHMAN, IN SUCH PRIVATE MOMENTS OF DEVOTION—A LESSON IN FAITH MORE POWERFUL THAN ANY SERMON I'D HEARD.

who had wagered everything on a dream—leaving behind a secure job in Ireland, a tight-knit extended family, and all that was familiar for an uncertain future in America.

The gamble proved harder than expected. With five kids, a much higher cost of living, and no support system, they found themselves stretched thin in ways they hadn't imagined. While my mom built her world through church, school activities, and community connections, Dad shouldered the financial burden silently, working endless hours and traveling whenever needed. His determination to make this leap of faith succeed pushed him forward, day after day, year after year.

The pressure of providing for five children and the isolation of life without any extended family or real friends took its toll on my father. During my middle school years, I watched him struggle to cope, creating strain in my parents' marriage despite their unwavering loyalty to each other. Yet even in this struggle, he taught me powerful lessons—first about life's complexities and then about strength of character when he worked through challenges through sheer determination, held by his commitment to remain dedicated to his family.

SAYING GOODBYE

Years later, Alzheimer's began eroding my father's memories, and our roles reversed. I became his go-to—managing his finances, serving as his power of attorney, and helping him navigate his progressive memory loss. Watching this proud man, who had sacrificed everything for his family's future, slowly slip away was super hard. But unlike most dementia patients, he never got angry or agitated. Even in his final days, he stayed loving and docile, his gentle spirit intact. In his final days, our entire family—24 of us, including spouses and 10 grandchildren—gathered for nearly 48 hours at his bedside, each of us honoring the remarkable man who had given us so much.

My dad's journey with Alzheimer's was a tremendous heartache for all of us. It was The Long Goodbye, as author Maureen Reagan described it in reference to her own father, former President Ronald Reagan. But through it all, our mom became an inspiration in her unfailing dedication to Dad right up to the end. As she spoon-fed him dinner every night, she taught us that in life's darkest moments, grace and devotion can transcend even the most powerful loss into a lesson about loyalty, love, and the true meaning of caregiving.

My mom died twenty years after my dad, as she lived—peacefully and fittingly in her sleep at age 92. Her lasting lesson was simple but powerful: you cannot feel good or be good by accident. While I may not follow her routines to such extremes, I have learned that structured habits create the bedrock for a grounded life.

THE LEGACY THEY LEFT

Looking back, I see how my parents' differences created not division but harmony in our home. As we've grown older, my siblings and I have come to recognize these differences as precious gifts. Mom's quiet grace and unwavering optimism, alongside Dad's joyful spontaneity and light-heartedness, weren't contradictions but complementary forces that balanced our family. Now, I find myself drawing on both their legacies—her structure when I need foundation and his humor when I need perspective. Together, they taught me to embrace each day with gratitude and to celebrate God's gifts, even on Seattle's cloudiest mornings. In their own unique ways, they built a foundation of love, sacrifice, and unwavering faith—a legacy that continues to light our way forward.

LESSONS LEARNED

- **FAITH LIVES IN THE QUIET MOMENTS—** My father kneeling by his hotel bed, my mother starting each day in prayer—they showed me that true faith isn't about grand gestures but about the private moments that shape who you become.

- **DISCIPLINE IS AN ACT OF LOVE—** Through Mom's meticulous routines and Dad's relentless work ethic, I learned that showing up consistently for the people you love is what matters most. Whether it's making school lunches or driving to late-night practices, dedication speaks louder than words.

- **JOY AND GRIT CAN COEXIST—**
  Mom could race a competitor to the finish line and laugh about it afterward, while Dad could face workplace pressures with a smile and an Irish joke. They taught me that life's challenges are easier when you don't take yourself too seriously.

- **COURAGE TAKES MANY FORMS—**
  It showed in Dad's leap of faith in leaving Ireland, in Mom's marathon training at 60, in their united front during tough times. They taught me that being brave isn't about being fearless—it's about moving forward anyway.

- **LOVE FINDS ITS OWN LANGUAGE—**
  Sometimes, it's a hot cup of tea delivered to your bedside. Other times, it's a secret trip to Dairy Queen. My parents showed me that love expresses itself in countless ways, but always with consistency and grace.

QUESTIONS FOR REFLECTION

1. Who you want to be (and who you do not want to be) are both valuable bookmarks in the story of your life. What did you learn from your parents that has helped shape you into the person you are today?

   _____

   _____

   _____

2. Which parent do you resemble more—a structured disciplinarian like my mother or a spontaneous free spirit like my father? How has this shaped your approach to challenges?

   _____

   _____

   _____

3. Think about other significant mentors from your childhood. Who was there for you—teaching, mentoring, nurturing, leading by example? What did you learn from them?

   _____

   _____

   _____

4. It can be tempting to blame the way we were brought up or point to disadvantages as "reasons" why others seem more successful than we are. But you have the choice. Two people can come from the exact same family, and one thrives, achieves, and lives in joy while the other complains, struggles, and is generally miserable. Which one are you? Are you who you want to be?

   _____

   _____

   _____

5. What small traditions or rituals from your childhood have you carried into adulthood?

   _____

   _____

   _____

6. Whether or not you are a parent, someone is watching you. You have friends, coworkers, and people you lead or mentor. What are they learning from you? Does what you say and what you do align? What are you modeling daily for those in your circle of influence?

   _____

   _____

   _____

7. If you've cared for someone who once cared for you, how did this reversal transform your relationship, and what did you discover about yourself in the process?

_____

_____

_____

8. What unexpected combination of traits do you carry from those who raised you? I got Mom's grit but Dad's love for celebration—what's your unique blend?

_____

_____

_____

9. Do you have someone to help hold you accountable to become the kind of person you want to be?

_____

_____

_____

f i v e

THE COMPATIBILITY CODE

"A successful marriage requires falling in love many times, always with the same person."

MIGNON MCLAUGHLIN

Before reconnecting with Sam, I dodged a lot of bullets—no disrespect to the great guys I dated in my twenties. Every one of those relationships taught me something. Without them, I wouldn't have figured out what really mattered to me, what I needed in a life partner, and—most importantly—who I was.

That's when I started to see it—balance wasn't the secret to a lasting relationship. It never was. Real love isn't about keeping score or splitting life evenly. It's about alignment. Knowing who you are, what matters most, and finding someone willing to build something with you, not around you.

Those years were the best training ground I could've asked for. If you're paying attention, dating in your twenties teaches you what you want, what you need, and what you're absolutely not willing to compromise on. Because for a partnership to thrive, you have to know yourself first. And then you have to take the time to understand your partner—to see if your values and visions actually align. When I was living in San Francisco right after college, a good friend shared something with me that would ultimately shape my approach to love and marriage. He had been dating, somewhat unsuccessfully, for a while. But then, over a casual lunch, he lit up as he told me about someone new. "This one's different," he said. "She checks all five boxes."

He called them "The Five Things"—five areas of compatibility that, in his view, made all the difference. As he explained each one, I felt an instant "aha" moment. It was like someone had handed me a framework for what I hadn't been able to articulate. I realized I had work to do—defining for myself what "good" looked like in each of those five areas, and how I would know when it was real. Up until that point, I'd experienced compatibility in two, maybe three of the five—but never in four, and certainly not all five.

There was one relationship in particular that really drove this home. On paper, it seemed perfect—we liked the same activities, had great chemistry, shared a friend group, and even talked about building a future together. But underneath it all, something was missing. I couldn't quite name it at the time, but I knew I couldn't picture us growing old together—let alone raising a family.

That relationship taught me the difference between connection and alignment. I didn't want someone who simply entertained me—I wanted someone with whom I could be completely myself. That clarity changed everything going forward.

Later, when Sam and I fell in love, we started using *the five things* as a lens to reflect on our own relationship. Over time, we gave it a name: THE COMPATIBILITY CODE.

The premise is simple—there are five core areas of compatibility that, when you're aligned on most of them, create a strong foundation for lasting connection, growth, and love over the long haul:

1. RECREATIONAL
2. SPIRITUAL
3. INTELLECTUAL
4. PHYSICAL
5. EMOTIONAL

When these areas align, the benefits are profound. Compatibility creates ease and harmony. It's not something you can manufacture, though it can absolutely be nurtured. It's something that feels natural—not forced. It deepens connection, builds a bond through shared values, and minimizes the misunderstandings that can drive couples apart. Alignment in these areas leads to greater happiness— those moments of joy and contentment that come from being with someone who truly "gets" you. And perhaps most importantly, it strengthens your commitment to each other. Compatibility gives you the long-haul resilience—the "we've got this" mindset that carries you through life's inevitable curveballs.

While compatibility is essential at the start of a relationship, sustaining it takes intention and awareness. As people, we are always evolving—our interests change, our values deepen, and our needs shift. The true power of "The Compatibility Code" lies not in finding perfect alignment from the start, but in the willingness to keep growing together, to keep choosing each other, and to nurture what you've built.

THE FIVE AREAS OF COMPATIBILITY

 ### AREA #1
RECREATIONAL COMPATIBILITY
How You Enjoy Spending Leisure Time Together

Recreational compatibility is about more than just being active—it's about how you enjoy spending your free time together. That might mean hiking, swimming, or skiing, but it can just as easily include visiting museums, exploring new restaurants, taking road trips, going to concerts, or simply spending a quiet evening cooking and talking. It's about whether you "enjoy doing life" together when the obligations are stripped away.

When Sam and I were first dating, our free time often meant exercise—running, tennis, skiing, or my attempts to surf alongside him. Our very first date set the tone: what was supposed to be a casual jog from my house in Madison Park turned into a six-mile run along Lake Washington. I remember running down Lake Washington Boulevard, the early fall temperatures still warm, with the lake glistening beside us. We talked about everything and nothing. There was an ease, a lightness that felt different. He wasn't racing me or two steps in front; he was just matching me stride for stride. I remember thinking, This is fun. He's fun. And for the first time in a long time, I didn't want the date to end.

Afterward, we had dinner at a cozy Italian café that became one of our favorite spots. That day sparked a rhythm of sharing interest and energy—sometimes moving, sometimes sitting still—but always connecting.

Over the years, we continued to explore and evolve how we spend time together. Sam taught me to ski (with varying success), and I coached him on swimming technique. One memorable early ski lesson ended with me throwing my poles down the mountain in a full-on meltdown—fortunately, Sam was far enough below not to hear my expletives. He just smiled and waited. That moment taught me something: I needed someone who could love me through both the graceful and the grumpy moments.

To be fair, I got my revenge during a long-distance lake swim. Sam, ever the optimist, joined me—only to end up grabbing my foot while I towed him to shore.

Today, our version of recreation looks different—long walks, yoga, or just relaxing on the couch while watching a new series. Sometimes it's an evening in cooking dinner or a Saturday afternoon shopping stores along South Congress in Austin. The activity matters less than the intention: dedicating time to be together, to talk, to laugh, and to enjoy each other's company without distraction—or phones!

Recreational compatibility isn't about doing all the same things—it's about being curious together, having fun in each other's presence, and finding joy in the everyday.

AREA #2
SPIRITUAL COMPATIBILITY
Shared Values, Beliefs, and Life Philosophies

While my upbringing was very traditional and Catholic, Sam's was less so, but he was always willing to support me in my faith journey. Before we got married, we were required to go through "Marriage Encounter" with the Catholic church—an experience I highly recommend because it brought up subjects we wouldn't have otherwise discussed. We explored important topics like the role of faith, tradition, and religion in our home. We talked about how we wanted to raise our kids, if they would be baptized, confirmed, and how we felt about attending weekly mass on Sundays.

While we didn't figure it all out in those meetings at the church, it did force us to pause, ponder, and share how we felt, which we had not done as specifically as answering those questions required. The most important outcome was that we aligned on the importance of a faith-filled home and our version of "Catholic-light." All three of our kids were baptized by my brother, who was a Jesuit priest, but they weren't confirmed. We didn't attend Sunday mass except for Christmas and Easter. Instead, we traded that for our time together on the ski mountain, in our RV, or just being together as a family. I am a big believer that God and faith can be practiced anywhere, not just in the "building," aka the church itself. Over the years, we have adapted a version of spirituality and faith that works for us as a couple, focusing more on spirituality than dogmatic formality.

 AREA #3
INTELLECTUAL COMPATIBILITY
Communication Styles, Interests, and Perspectives

Sam is much more well-read and intellectual than I am, and of the five things, this is where we are the most different. Sam is fascinated by history, politics, and legal-related issues, while I find myself gravitating toward business, fashion, health and wellness. What keeps us compatible is that we are both interested in the other person's interests. Sam may get me to watch a history documentary, and I am constantly sharing articles about longevity, but we respect each other's interests enough to make time to listen and learn from each other. We share a genuine curiosity in discovering new things, challenging ourselves, and finding mental stimulation as a balance to the day-to-day routine.

One of our most meaningful shared experiences in this area came when we joined an organization focused on economic issues, global security, and education. At first, I wasn't sure it would be my thing—those topics didn't sound nearly as appealing to me as fashion, food, or fitness. But I quickly came to appreciate the depth and challenge of the conversations we were having, both with other members and with each other.

Each month, we attended events featuring speakers on big-picture topics shaping the world. The discussions stretched me—they were outside my usual lane—but they sparked something new. We'd come home energized, trading takeaways and insights with each other and, eventually, with our kids. The experience made a lasting impression on our family—so much so that our daughter Declan became the organization's first intern at just 15.

What began as an area of potential disconnect turned into one of our strongest bonds. It was a powerful reminder that intellectual compatibility isn't about sharing all the same interests—it's about respecting each other's passions, staying curious, and being willing to grow together.

 AREA #4
PHYSICAL COMPATIBILITY
Intimacy, Affection, and Physical Connection

In your twenties, physical compatibility tends to be over-emphasized. You're young, energetic, and often measuring passion by intensity. But as you grow older, you realize that intimacy is less about sparks and more about a different kind of connection. Physicality will inevitably evolve, but the need for closeness never really goes away—it just shifts in form.

Like exercise, your physical relationship changes with the seasons of life. Maybe you're not running six miles anymore, but you're still holding hands on long walks. The key is staying intentional—keeping connection alive through both effort and affection.

We've always tried to make this part of our relationship a priority. During the busiest years—raising kids, managing careers, juggling life—we learned about a little ritual called "Tune-Up Tuesdays." It was a way of keeping intimacy from falling to the bottom of the to-do list. Life was chaotic, but this simple weekly check-in reminded us that we mattered—not just as partners, but as lovers, too.

According to Sam, three things helped our consistency:

1. We slept in a queen-sized bed until only recently.
2. We never had a TV in our bedroom (also until recently).
3. And—we've always slept naked.

Smaller bed, no distractions, and already undressed? Let's just say it helped keep the spark alive.

In all seriousness, physical compatibility isn't just about sex. It's about knowing how to express love through touch, affection, and presence. It's the long hug after a hard day, a gentle kiss before going to sleep every night, the quiet knowing that you're still each other's person.

Physical intimacy will look different at 50 than it did at 30—but it doesn't have to lose its importance. If anything, it becomes more meaningful because it's built on years of trust, vulnerability, and shared history. That kind of connection doesn't just happen—it's created, nurtured, and redefined again and again.

AREA #5 EMOTIONAL COMPATIBILITY
Understanding Each Other's Emotional Needs and Responses

Emotional compatibility might be the hardest to define—but it's arguably the most essential of all five areas. Getting married in our thirties helped us tremendously in this department. By then, we had each experienced the full spectrum of relationships, breakups, and the hard-earned lessons that come with them.

Neither of us is overly emotional—we're generally calm and levelheaded—but we're different in meaningful ways, especially when it comes to how we express love. (Sam's love language is physical connection; mine is acts of service.) Our communication style tends to be cool and rational; we're not yellers or screamers, though I quickly learned that arguing with a lawyer presents its own unique challenges!

I vividly remember one night when this difference between us showed up in the most meaningful way. My dad was declining with Alzheimer's, and I didn't realize just how emotionally exhausted I was—until I walked into the kitchen and started crying at the counter. I felt like I was carrying everything: work, kids, caregiving. Sam didn't try to fix it. He didn't offer a solution or a pep talk. He just stood beside me, wrapped his arm around me, and said, "I'm right here with you. You don't have to do it alone."

It wasn't grand—it was quiet, steady love.

Over the years, we've learned when to dig in our heels and when to let go. But more importantly, we've learned to lean into each other when it matters most, always grounded in mutual respect. Even in our toughest disagreements, we've never used the "F-word" or called each other names. Sure, we've had stormy moments, but we keep our emotions in check enough to make reconciliation not only possible—but easier.

Over time, we've developed an unspoken language of support. We instinctively know when the other needs encouragement, space, distraction, or simply a quiet presence. It's not perfect, but it's deeply attuned. And if I had to name the most important compatibility of all—it would be this one. Emotional compatibility is the glue that connects all the others. Without it, the rest begins to unravel. With it, everything else becomes stronger.

MAINTAINING COMPATIBILITY THROUGH CHANGE

Life doesn't stand still—and neither do relationships. The version of Sam I married isn't the same man he is today, just as I'm not the same woman he married. We've both evolved—sometimes in expected ways, and other times in ways that surprised us, with new interests, shifting perspectives, and changing needs.

There were times when I wondered if we were growing in different directions. I remember one Sunday, sitting in our living room across from one another, feeling disconnected and disheartened. We weren't really communicating about anything substantive, and things felt "off" – like we were trading logistics and to-dos. I looked at Sam and said quietly, "I miss us." Without hesitation, he came to my side, squeezed my hand, and said, "Me too. Let's fix it."

That moment reminded me that compatibility isn't about having the perfect puzzle pieces—it's about choosing, again and again, to put them together. To keep showing up. To keep choosing "us."

That choice—to be honest, vulnerable, and willing to evolve together—has been a guiding principle throughout our marriage. Over time, we've found three key practices that help us keep compatibility alive as we grow and change:

- FIRST, we prioritize updating our understanding of each other regularly. Just like you'd update a business plan—or the throw pillows on your couch (which, let's be honest, I do more often than necessary)—relationships need refreshing, too. This means asking questions that go beyond daily logistics: What's been inspiring you lately? What's been hard? What feels different than it did a year ago? These conversations help us stay in sync, even as we evolve individually.

- SECOND, we've learned to adapt our relationship skills as life stages shift. When we became parents, we were thrown into the chaos of sleep deprivation, divided attention, and entirely new demands. Our time together shrank dramatically. The things that once came easily—spontaneous dates, recreational activities, long conversations—required intention. So, we pivoted. We focused on quality over quantity, reminding each other that this season, like all the others, would pass. And it did.

- THIRD, we've adjusted our expectations across all five compatibility areas. Physical connection at 50 doesn't look like it did at 30, but it's no less meaningful. Our intellectual connection has deepened with life experience. And spiritual compatibility has grown as we've faced bigger life questions. Instead of clinging to what these things "used to" look like, we've learned to embrace how they show up in this season of life.

The beauty of growing together is that you discover new versions of compatibility you couldn't have imagined when you first met. Today, Sam and I enjoy interests in our fifties that weren't even on our radar in our thirties—creating fresh connection even after 25 years of marriage. Back then, date night meant great outfits, reservations, and a fabulous cocktail. Now, it's sweats, a movie on the couch, and a mocktail. And somehow, those quiet nights feel just as special and romantic—maybe even more so—because they're wrapped in history, comfort, and a love that keeps evolving.

THE CODE AS A GUIDE, NOT A RULE

The Compatibility Code isn't a checklist or a formula for marital success—it's a compass. It's helped Sam and me navigate 25 years of ups and downs, not because we're perfectly aligned in all five areas (we're not), but because we've learned to grow together where it matters most.

Love alone doesn't make a relationship last, but love combined with compatibility creates something extraordinary. Over the years, our alignment has shifted, and life's challenges have tested every part of our connection. What carried us through wasn't perfection—it was our continued choice to keep showing up for each other.

Like a garden, compatibility needs tending. What flourished last year might need more care today. One way we stay connected is through our "Quarterly Connection Check-ins"—Sunday morning coffee chats where we take turns sharing how we're feeling about work, family, health, our relationship, and even sex. It sounds formal, but it's become a grounding ritual. We don't always hit every quarter, but when we do, we feel more aligned—more connected to each other—and it makes the day-to-day conversations much more substantive and real.

Looking back, I'm convinced that understanding these five areas gave us something even more valuable than certainty—it gave us a shared language. A way to course correct, to reconnect, and to keep choosing each other through every season.

We're not the same couple we were when we first fell in love—and that's the point. We've grown, stumbled, forgiven, and grown again. What makes it work isn't perfect alignment, but a shared commitment to keep evolving—together.

Compatibility isn't a destination. It's a choice. A beautiful, messy, ever-evolving code you write together, one season at a time.

LESSONS LEARNED

- **KNOWING YOURSELF IS PARAMOUNT—** Understanding yourself—your values, needs, and non-negotiables—is essential before you can truly align with someone else.

- **COMPATIBILITY GOES BEYOND CHEMISTRY—**
  While initial attraction matters, lasting relationships require alignment in multiple dimensions: recreational, spiritual, intellectual, physical, and emotional.

- **ADAPTATION IS KEY—**
  Even with strong compatibility, relationships require flexibility and willingness to evolve and grow together.

- **RESPECT DIFFERENCES—**
  Different interests can strengthen rather than weaken a relationship when approached with mutual respect and curiosity.

- **INTENTIONALITY MATTERS—**
  Creating traditions like "Tune-Up Tuesday" helped us deliberately maintain a connection vs. just passively hoping we would.

- **IT'S NOT WHAT YOU SAY; IT'S HOW YOU SAY IT—**
  Sam and I always try to maintain our composure when we disagree, never using harsh words at each other and keeping our cool.

- **PRIOR RELATIONSHIPS MATTER—**
  Your relationships in your twenties reveal what is critical to you and prepare you for a stronger partnership later.

QUESTIONS FOR REFLECTION

1. In which of the five compatibility areas do you and your partner align most strongly? Which area might benefit from more attention and growth?

   _____

   _____

   _____

2. How have your shared activities evolved throughout your relationship? What new forms of recreational compatibility might you explore as you continue to age together?

   _____

   _____

   _____

3. What values and beliefs form the foundation of your spiritual compatibility? Have these evolved over time, and if so, how?

   _____

   _____

   _____

4. How do you navigate intellectual differences with your partner? Do you see these differences as strengths or challenges?

_____

_____

_____

5. What intentional practices have you created to maintain your physical connection with each other through different life stages? What adjustments might be necessary in the future?

_____

_____

_____

6. How would you describe your emotional language as a couple? What unspoken signals help you understand when your partner needs support?

_____

_____

_____

7. Looking at your past relationships, what compatibility lessons did they teach you that you've applied to your current partnership?

_____

_____

_____

8. Which aspect of The Compatibility Code was most surprising or insightful to you? Why?

_____

_____

_____

BALANCE IS BULLSHIT

LOVE ALONE DOESN'T MAKE A
RELATIONSHIP LAST,
BUT LOVE COMBINED WITH
COMPATIBILITY CREATES
SOMETHING EXTRAORDINARY.

s i x

TRADING PLACES

"Do not go where the path may lead, go instead where there is no path and leave a trail."

RALPH WALDO EMERSON

CLIMBING THE HILL TO A NEW CHAPTER

Most couples debate about chores, money, or in-laws. We certainly did, but in 2000, we debated a new topic: which one of us would leave a promising career to raise our child? We were less than two years into our marriage and thrilled to be expecting our first child. The answer to this new topic would reshape our marriage and challenge everything we thought we knew about modern parenthood.

"Doll, guess what?"

"What?" Sam asked.

"I'm pregnant!"

Shortly after our wedding, we experienced a miscarriage, so my announcement was welcomed. We were thrilled—even if a little nervous—to be expecting a child again.

As the youngest in my family, I had plenty of experience with five nephews and two nieces, while Sam had a niece and another on the way. We had watched our siblings navigate parenthood differently—my eldest sister with a full-time nanny, my other sister using daycare while continuing her nursing career. Sam's sister was a pilot, and she chose to take a leave of absence until her girls were old enough for preschool and daycare.

"What do you think we should do about childcare?" I asked Sam casually but without any real urgency. The demands of my job seemed much more pressing at the time.

"Let's read the next chapter," was more common as we were reading *The Secret of the Baby Whisperer* together, alternating reading out loud so the baby could get used to Sam's voice. This makes me laugh now, as if the baby couldn't hear him every other minute of the day. Reading this book was a bedtime ritual and our training course for what it was like to have our own baby. We were learning all kinds of tips and tricks about creating good sleep habits, daily schedules, and how to "integrate the baby into our life."

Sam and I both came from traditional households with stay-at-home mothers, but ironically, we never talked about me staying home. We didn't talk much about childcare at all until the third trimester of my pregnancy.

A WALK THAT CHANGED EVERYTHING

At around 30 weeks pregnant, we were taking one of our long, slow neighborhood walks. I was at that point where any incline at all made my heart pound, and I was instantly out of breath. It didn't matter what kind of shape I was in – I was 180 lbs and panting like I had just swam a 100-meter sprint.

"Wait," I gasped, bending over and holding my lower back, "let me just catch my breath for a second."

"Sure, no problem, take as long as you need," Sam said.

"Oh my God," I said, "I actually cannot imagine getting any larger ... and I still have 10 more weeks!"

"You're doing great, love," Sam said. Always my biggest cheerleader.

I caught my breath, and we got back to flat ground.

"What do you think we should do for childcare after my maternity leave is over?" I asked.

"I don't know," Sam shook his head, "I haven't really thought about it yet. How long can you take for maternity leave?"

"Four months," I replied.

"Hmmm. Well, I also get four months, so we can overlap a bit ... it would be fun to have a couple of months together."

"That would be great. Maybe we could go somewhere warm?"

"Yes, I could ask my parents if they would be interested so we would have a little help from them, too."

"Love that idea!" we walked a little further, each lost in our own thoughts, "but what about after all of that? Then what do you think we should do?"

Sam put his hand on the small of my back and touched my elbow to steady me as we walked. "I think I'd prefer to have a nanny in our house if possible, and if we could afford it," I said, "it would just make the logistics before and after work much easier."

I assumed I was going back to work.

"I agree," Sam nodded.

"But," I continued, "I am not sure I like the idea of a nanny 'raising' our kids."

Immediately, Sam echoed, "Me either."

At that moment, it was clear to both of us, and we agreed that, ideally, one of us should stay home rather than have a full-time nanny or put our children in daycare.

"So, how do we make that work?" I asked, slowing once more to catch my breath.

"I love my job," Sam said, "but realistically, there is very little room for me to make any more money. You love your job, too, and working for a big company like Nordstrom seems like a much smarter bet than the government. And you are doing so well—you keep getting recognized and winning awards. Aren't you getting a big bonus this year, too?"

"Yes," I panted, "and I really do love it."

"You know," Sam offered, "I've heard of a few people recently doing a job share at the prosecutor's office after they've had kids. One person works two days a week while the other works three days per week. I could see if that would be an option for me."

I looked over at him in wonder, knowing what a rare treasure I had in him. Sam loved his job as a county deputy prosecutor, but in this moment, I realized he was willing to pause his career for the love of me and our family—the ultimate statement of commitment.

> I REALIZED HE WAS WILLING TO PAUSE HIS CAREER FOR THE LOVE OF ME AND OUR FAMILY—THE ULTIMATE STATEMENT OF COMMITMENT.

"I could stay home with the baby three days a week, and we could get a nanny for the other two days. How does that sound?"

"Really??" I looked at him in disbelief, "You would be willing to do that?"

As we continued our walk, we talked through what his part-time job and a nanny would look like. In reality, we had no idea. What we did know was that we were aligned on our values. Having one parent at home with our baby was the most important factor, and we were both willing to do whatever it took to ensure that. While my career path wasn't entirely clear, we knew I had good earning potential working at a large company. Sam's trajectory was steady and predictable, but his earning potential was known and limited because he worked for the government.

By the time we returned to our house, we had a plan.

Sam needed to get approval, and eventually, we needed to find a nanny, but I still had 10 more weeks to go. In the weeks that followed, as I approached my delivery date, I occasionally questioned whether we'd made the right choice.

"Wait, are you sure *I* shouldn't be the one to stay home?" or "Why do *you* get to stay home and I don't?" I would ask. Memories of my mother bringing tea to my bed every morning filled me with nostalgia. *Am I a bad mother if I work and let Sam take care of the baby?*

UNEXPECTED CONFIRMATION

About six weeks before Declan was born and roughly a month after our hillside discussion, Pete Nordstrom walked into my office with a game-changing offer to promote me to Vice President, Corporate Merchandise Manager position, going from overseeing $75M to $250 million P&L. At just 34 years old and about to become a first-time mother, I became the youngest officer in Nordstrom company history.

Pete's offer seemed like confirmation that choosing my career was right for our family.

Declan arrived on February 11, 2001. Sam was in the midst of a murder trial and couldn't take time off that first week, though he managed to sleep in the hospital room those first two nights, heading to court each morning. Thank goodness for Sam's parents' support during those early, sleepless days.

Once we found our rhythm, I embraced this unprecedented break—my first of three in 12 years at Nordstrom. No emails, no voicemails, no cell phone. Just long walks with Declan and a much-needed reset.

After ten weeks, work started calling me back. My assistant began dropping off reports during those rare moments of downtime, and slowly, I reconnected with the world I'd stepped away from. When Sam's paternity leave began at three months, we shared one glorious month together as a family.

MRS. EXECUTIVE AND MR. MOM

June marked my return to work, and the timing felt right. Any longer might have made it impossible, as Declan was just starting to sleep through the night, and our days were becoming magical. I often tell expecting mothers to be mindful about leave duration if they plan to return to work. There's a window—wait too long, and going back to work becomes heart-wrenching.

I can honestly say that I returned to work with a sense of ease, grateful beyond measure that Sam would be home with Declan most of the week. He was eager to start his new role as "Mr. Mom," even if he didn't quite know what he was in for, and I remember other dads telling him that they would *love* to trade places with their wives "in a second!" I suspected most just saw it as an easy escape from their jobs without understanding the real demands of full-time parenting. Notably, not one of them ever followed suit. There were very few stay-at-home dads anywhere back then. Sam was the trailblazer and, realistically speaking, much more suited to this role than I ever was.

LESSONS LEARNED

When making decisions, remember these guiding principles:

- TRUST YOUR PARTNERSHIP—
  Values matter more than traditional roles. When Sam and I faced our childcare decision, we focused on what would work best for our family rather than what society expected.

into my office with a game-changing offer to promote me to Vice President, Corporate Merchandise Manager position, going from overseeing $75M to $250 million P&L. At just 34 years old and about to become a first-time mother, I became the youngest officer in Nordstrom company history.

Pete's offer seemed like confirmation that choosing my career was right for our family.

Declan arrived on February 11, 2001. Sam was in the midst of a murder trial and couldn't take time off that first week, though he managed to sleep in the hospital room those first two nights, heading to court each morning. Thank goodness for Sam's parents' support during those early, sleepless days.

Once we found our rhythm, I embraced this unprecedented break—my first of three in 12 years at Nordstrom. No emails, no voicemails, no cell phone. Just long walks with Declan and a much-needed reset.

After ten weeks, work started calling me back. My assistant began dropping off reports during those rare moments of downtime, and slowly, I reconnected with the world I'd stepped away from. When Sam's paternity leave began at three months, we shared one glorious month together as a family.

MRS. EXECUTIVE AND MR. MOM

June marked my return to work, and the timing felt right. Any longer might have made it impossible, as Declan was just starting to sleep through the night, and our days were becoming magical. I often tell expecting mothers to be mindful about leave duration if they plan to return to work. There's a window—wait too long, and going back to work becomes heart-wrenching.

I can honestly say that I returned to work with a sense of ease, grateful beyond measure that Sam would be home with Declan most of the week. He was eager to start his new role as "Mr. Mom," even if he didn't quite know what he was in for, and I remember other dads telling him that they would *love* to trade places with their wives "in a second!" I suspected most just saw it as an easy escape from their jobs without understanding the real demands of full-time parenting. Notably, not one of them ever followed suit. There were very few stay-at-home dads anywhere back then. Sam was the trailblazer and, realistically speaking, much more suited to this role than I ever was.

LESSONS LEARNED

When making decisions, remember these guiding principles:

- **TRUST YOUR PARTNERSHIP—**
  Values matter more than traditional roles. When Sam and I faced our childcare decision, we focused on what would work best for our family rather than what society expected.

This trust in each other's strengths allowed us to create our own unique path forward.

- **COURAGE TO BE DIFFERENT—** Breaking from convention requires both confidence and conviction. By supporting Sam as a stay-at-home dad in 2001 when it was rare, we learned that the right choice isn't always the most common one—it's the one that aligns with your family's needs.

- **COMMUNICATE EARLY—** Don't wait for deadlines to discuss life-changing decisions. While we were fortunate that our values aligned naturally during that hillside conversation, having these important discussions early on gives couples time to explore options and align expectations.

- **SUPPORT EACH OTHER'S ROLES—** Success in nontraditional arrangements depends on mutual respect and encouragement. I learned to champion Sam's role as primary caregiver while he fully supported my career advancement—creating a foundation of trust that made our choice work.

QUESTIONS FOR REFLECTION

1. Think about your definition of partnership. How has it evolved from what you initially expected or what you witnessed growing up?

　

　

　

2. How do you and your partner make major life decisions? What values guide these conversations?

　

　

　

3. Consider the most significant conversation you've had with your partner about roles and responsibilities. What surprised you about each other's perspectives?

TRADING PLACES

4. Consider a time when you had to trust your partner's judgment even when it went against conventional wisdom. What gave you the confidence to move forward?

_____

_____

_____

5. Reflect on a moment when you had to weigh career advancement against family priorities. How did you navigate that decision?

_____

_____

_____

6. Think about a time when you chose to break from traditional expectations. What fears did you have to overcome? How did that decision shape your path?

_____

_____

_____

7. Reflect on the role models who shaped your views of family and career. How have you chosen to either follow or diverge from their examples?

_____

_____

_____

seven

THREE PREGNANCIES AND THREE PROMOTIONS

"We can do hard things, not because we are extraordinary, but because we are designed to rise."

GLENNON DOYLE

FIRST TIME AROUND
A NEW ROLE, A NEW REALITY

There's never a perfect time to tell your boss you're pregnant. But there I was—a newly promoted VP overseeing a $250M business—about to share news that would reshape both my career and my life.

What I didn't know then was that this would be the first of three such moments, each arriving at an increasingly critical point in my career.

After speaking to a group of young female entrepreneurs, one of them came to me and said, "Tell me what it was really like." Leaning in, Ellie's eyes were full of genuine curiosity. "Being pregnant while running a business that size—how did you handle it all?"

I smiled, remembering how my hands had trembled before that first conversation.

"You know, it's funny looking back now. When I first shared the news, I thought I had it all mapped out perfectly: a big new job, a $250M P&L, a strong team, and a great husband. On paper, it seemed manageable."

"Were you scared?" she asked.

"Terrified," I admitted, laughing softly. "And here's something I rarely tell people—I didn't love being pregnant the way some women do. The morning sickness, the constant exhaustion … I felt guilty about that for a long time. Like somehow, I was failing at both pregnancy and leadership."

As a fashion executive and lifelong athlete, I was used to being in control—of my body, my schedule, and my team. Pregnancy changed all that.

The "pregnancy brain" was real and all-consuming. I found myself losing my train of thought mid-meeting, showing up on the wrong day for appointments, and writing down every detail I could no longer trust myself to remember. Ironically, that made our maternity coverage plans even stronger.

Until then, I could outwork anyone in the room. Now, I was practically dozing off mid-meeting.

Ellie raised her eyebrows, and I laughed. "Want to know how bad it got? I once parked my car for a meeting and had to recline my seat for a twenty-minute nap just to make it through."

"But you found ways to cope?" she asked, picking up on my shift in tone.

"Yes. I reminded myself that pregnancy is a privilege, not an illness—and that adapting didn't mean giving up who I was."

She nodded, and I continued.

About six weeks before my due date, Pete Nordstrom came into my office with unexpected news.

"I'd like you to oversee the Contemporary department along with Juniors," he said. "The timing's not ideal, but

I REMINDED MYSELF THAT PREGNANCY IS A PRIVILEGE, NOT AN ILLNESS— AND THAT ADAPTING DIDN'T MEAN GIVING UP WHO I WAS.

you're the right person for the job. Just do what you can before your baby comes."

It would nearly double my business overnight to almost $500M.

Those next six weeks were intense. While most expectant mothers were winding down, I was in Los Angeles conducting high-stakes vendor negotiations.

I treated my baby bump as casually as a new haircut, staying focused on strengthening vendor relationships and documenting every critical metric and decision point.

I wasn't just preparing for maternity leave—I was fortifying the business to thrive without me.

Three days before my due date, I woke up feeling different. Still, I insisted on going into the office to wrap up loose ends. There I sat at my desk, Sam perched in the chair by my office door, while every seven or eight minutes, I winced through contractions. Finally, I hit send on my last email, and we walked to the parking garage.

Declan was born that night at 11 p.m.

I took four months off—and completely checked out from work. That freedom didn't happen by accident.

I'd created detailed responsibility maps outlining everything from daily operations to vendor negotiations, with timelines, key decisions, and potential pitfalls flagged. I empowered my team to lead, not just fill gaps. Pete Nordstrom checked in directly with them, giving my leaders invaluable executive exposure. When I returned, the business wasn't just intact—it was stronger.

Ellie shook her head in amazement. "You didn't just hold the line—you grew it while you were out."

I smiled. "Maternity leave wasn't a setback. It was a setup—for growth."

THE SECOND TIME
HIGHER STAKES, STRONGER SYSTEMS

Just twelve months after returning, I found out I was pregnant again. While I'd always wanted my kids close in age, the timing took me by surprise—and the familiar wave of anxiety washed over me. But this time, I had a playbook.

Before sharing the news, I mapped out the next year's major decisions and quietly shifted relationships to rising leaders.

When I finally told my team, the shock on their faces was unmistakable.

Hank was born just twenty months after Declan. I again took four months off—this time during the critical fourth quarter. Retailers live and die by the holiday season, and the pressure to leave an airtight plan was immense. But my team delivered a strong finish to the year, proving that good systems and trust in leadership could beat any holiday chaos.

Ellie laughed. "Did you even have time to *be* shocked with that second one?"

"Not really," I grinned. "We just poured another cup of coffee—or glass of wine—and kept going."

THE SURPRISE THIRD
NEW LIFE, NEW OPPORTUNITIES

Life has a way of surprising you with its best gifts.

During a planning meeting, I couldn't focus—my brain fogged, my appetite raging. I whispered to my finance manager that I might be pregnant.

That evening, a positive test confirmed what my body had already suspected.

Sam paced the house that night, clutching a glass of straight vodka, muttering about how we'd manage—and where we'd even put another child. We ended up converting the garage into a playroom, and Ashleigh turned out to be the best unplanned blessing we could have imagined.

By my third pregnancy announcement in less than four years, I had learned to read the room. I walked into those conversations with hard-earned confidence, armed with proof that executive leadership and motherhood weren't mutually exclusive.

A week before my due date, I sat down with Pete Nordstrom, expecting our usual transition review. Instead, he interrupted me:

THREE PREGNANCIES AND THREE PROMOTIONS

"That all sounds great, but what I really want to talk to you about is something else."

"When you get back, I'd like you to take over all of Women's Wear."

I stared at him.

"All of it?" I blurted, my mind racing.

Tripling my business responsibility—from $500M to over $1.5B—while raising three kids under four?

I smiled weakly.

"Well...maybe I should have this baby first and follow up with you in a bit."

Deep down, I knew two things: he needed me, and I was competitive enough to want it.

But right then, I was overwhelmed—and grateful Pete gave me the space to process a career-defining moment without pressure.

True to his word, Pete honored my maternity leave. No calls. No emails. Just the rare gift of complete disconnection—something I had learned to protect fiercely. Back then, before cell phones tethered us constantly, I even disabled my email and voicemail for my first leave. By my third, I kept my access active but barely touched it, too consumed by the beautiful chaos of three little ones. Three months later, I asked my assistant to bring over reports.

Then, over coffee, while the baby napped, Pete and I began deep dives into reshaping a $1.5B division—and reshaping my life.

Each conversation left me both exhilarated and terrified. Could I triple my responsibility...while tripling the number of car seats in our minivan?

COMING BACK
STEPPING INTO THE STORM

> FEAR ISN'T A STOP SIGN— IT'S JUST A SIGNAL YOU'RE ABOUT TO GROW.

Coming back wasn't just returning to work—it was stepping into a perfect storm. I eased back strategically, a few days a week at first, giving myself space to recalibrate.

Ellie leaned forward again. "Were you scared you couldn't do it?"

I paused, then answered honestly. "Yes. Every single day. But fear isn't a stop sign—it's just a signal you're about to grow."

Because I wasn't just the same executive returning to the same job, I was a mother of three now—and that changed everything about how I worked, thought, and led. At 38, I was taking on the largest role in the company while navigating the most demanding chapter of motherhood. Some days, I fired on all cylinders. Other days, I struggled to find my footing. Gradually, I found my new normal.

LESSONS FROM THE JUGGLE
REDEFINING LEADERSHIP AND SUCCESS

The juggle between executive life and motherhood taught me that leadership isn't about being superhuman—it's about being real, adaptable, and resilient.

The emotional landscape is complex: the mom guilt, the pressure, the fear of shortchanging either side. But these feelings aren't signs of weakness—they're proof that you care deeply about both.

For any woman wondering if you can do both:

Yes, you absolutely can.

Just remember:

Your path doesn't have to look like anyone else's.

Build your support system. Trust your team.

And give yourself grace along the way.

Because here's the truth:

Balance is bullshit.

There were no perfectly even scales during those years. There was no magic formula where work and motherhood politely took turns.

There was chaos. There was joy. There was exhaustion and exhilaration—often in the same day.

And somehow, through it all, I didn't just survive. I grew.

I built a life where career and family could both thrive—not because it was balanced, but because it was real.

LESSONS LEARNED

- **PREPARATION CREATES POSSIBILITY—** Strategic maternity leave planning isn't just about continuity—it's about building leadership strength across the team. The true measure of a leader isn't what happens in their presence, but what happens in their absence.

- **REWRITE THE RULES—** Your limitations are often self-imposed. Sometimes, the biggest opportunities arrive at the most inconvenient times. Growth and adaptation are not mutually exclusive.

- **EMBRACE THE JOURNEY—** Neither motherhood nor leadership follows a straight line. Staying flexible without losing sight of your goals is the real secret to thriving through change.

- **REDEFINE YOUR BEST—**
  Your best looks different in different seasons—and that's okay. Success isn't about constant peak performance. It's about impact, adaptability, and outcomes.

QUESTIONS FOR REFLECTION

1. Think about a time when you faced what seemed like competing life goals. How did you challenge your assumptions about what was possible?

   _____

   _____

   _____

2. How has your definition of "having it all" evolved as your life circumstances have changed?

   _____

   _____

   _____

3. When has an apparent obstacle turned into an unexpected opportunity for you? What mindset shifts made that possible?

BALANCE IS BULLSHIT

_____

_____

_____

4. What does your current support system look like—and how might you strengthen it?

_____

_____

_____

5. How do you measure success today? How would it change if you measured it by how well things run in your absence, not just your presence?

_____

_____

_____

eight

BALANCING BABIES, BILLIONS, AND BOUNDARIES

"Ginger Rogers did everything Fred Astaire did. She just did it backwards and in high heels."

ANN RICHARDS, 45TH GOVERNOR OF TEXAS

THE MYTH OF PERFECT BALANCE

When you have young kids and a big job, there is no balance. It's more like survival mode while investing in the future. It's basically boot camp. But when you're doing something hard with someone you love for the most important things in the world, you'll surprise yourself at what you can accomplish.

A DAY IN THE LIFE

My alarm jolts me awake at 5:00 a.m. out of a dead sleep. I crawl out of bed, put on my swimsuit and sweats, and by 5:30 a.m., I'm diving into the pool for a master's workout. By 6:45 a.m., I'm racing back home with a towel wrapped around my dripping hair. I make a cup of coffee and head to my bathroom to blow-dry my hair and attempt to put on makeup at the same time—every minute counts.

I'm dressed and as ready as I'm going to be by 7:30 a.m. when I go from room to room to wake the kids. One of my favorite parts of the day—their messy hair and bodies strewn about their beds with a scratchy little voice, "Hi mama," is just the best way to start my day, not to mention it gives Sam a few minutes of solitude to enjoy his cup of coffee in peace. A few minutes later, we all meet in the kitchen, where Sam is flipping pancakes or pouring cereal. I call out a couple of reminders his way, then kiss each small head goodbye with wishes for a wonderful day.

Eight minutes later, midway across the bridge, I call Sam from my cell with a few more reminders. I navigate downtown Seattle's streets at speed, occasionally leaving my car idling at the employee entrance for my assistant to park so I am not late for the 8:00 a.m. executive meeting.

My day becomes a blur of meetings, my assistant walking beside me, preparing me with necessary reports and updates. I move through the 6th floor until lunchtime, when I hit the employee café for a run through the salad bar and then return to my desk to devour my "lunch" between emails.

The afternoon fills with vendor meetings about financial plans and performance reviews, product development presentations for upcoming seasons, one-on-one sessions with my divisional leaders, and then signing off on the holiday marketing campaign.

By 5:00 p.m., I've barely paused to drink water or use the restroom. Not the healthiest day, but I did at least get my workout in. After quickly organizing papers on my desk, I'm back in the car, crossing the bridge. I call Sam again, confirming he's packed everything for the swim meet—extra towels, sweats, snacks, and dinner for a cold, rainy evening.

I rush into the house and upstairs, barely greeting anyone, changing into clothes suitable for a long, wet evening at the swim club. We return home by 9, tuck the kids into bed, unpack the car, and load soggy towels and sweats into the dryer. Then I head upstairs to pack for tomorrow morning's flight to a new store opening. By 10-ish, the day is done, and I collapse into bed, setting the alarm for another whirlwind day tomorrow.

THE FOUNDATION FOR SUCCESS

People often ask me how I determined the "perfect time" to have children while building a career. The truth is, there isn't one. What matters is building your foundation first–aligning with your partner on starting a family and understanding priorities as a couple and as a new family.

It's about proving your value at work so you don't feel like you have to look over your shoulder and doubt if you're being judged when you need to focus on your family. It's about developing your team so that when you need to, you can rely on them, and they will make you look good. And most importantly, it's about creating systems in every aspect of your life. Don't wait for the perfect moment; prepare for the moment you choose.

THE HOW-TO

Unlike most big challenges in life, like running a marathon, climbing a mountain, or doing an Ironman triathlon, there is no training plan or blueprint for managing the days and years of juggling career ambition with a young family. It's kind of like being thrown into the deep end of the pool, and somehow you figure it out and get to shore alive, albeit exhausted and even a bit traumatized.

As I look back on it now, with a nice hot cup of coffee in my hand, sitting by the fire looking out the window, I sometimes can't believe what I did—what *we* did during those years. I often say "I was a machine" at work–so hyper-efficient with meetings, conversations, and decisions, for fear I would, God forbid, waste a minute. I was organized and efficient. I had to be to get it all done.

But I wasn't a control freak, and I think that is what enabled me to be successful in my career. I trusted Sam implicitly and learned to let things go—like a slightly messy house, funny outfits designed and worn by the kids, owning a minivan, and showing up to work with one navy and one black shoe on—yes, that's what happens when you get dressed in the dark and in a hurry.

The biggest advice I can give is that you need to put systems in place. Here's how:

IT STARTS WITH SELF-PRESERVATION

Self-preservation is different than self-care and should not be confused with being selfish. If you don't take care of yourself, there's no way you can show up for your partner, children, or team.

I'm a big believer in starting each day on your toes, ready for action, not on your heels reacting to chaos. This could be just five minutes of deep breathing, ending your shower with cold water, or quickly reading something inspiring. Before important meetings, I carved out fifteen minutes to center myself. It doesn't need to be elaborate—just a moment to signal to yourself that "you got this."

These small moments compound over time. On my most hectic mornings, skipping this brief ritual left me off-balance all day—proof that the smallest investments often yield the greatest returns.

The rest is about essentials—sleep, decent food, water, and fitness. Being busy isn't an excuse for being unhealthy. I watched colleagues subsist on coffee, never exercise, and then wonder why they weren't firing on all cylinders or were burned out by mid-afternoon. The fancy self-care routines can wait for later in life—for now, just nail the basics.

CALENDAR MANAGEMENT

If something is important to you, put it on your calendar. I often tell people, "If you want to know what I'm doing next Tuesday at 3:00 p.m., I'll show you my calendar. It's walking my dog." Not that I would ever miss walking my dog, but the point is, everything that matters, that needs to happen in a day, is on my calendar. It's an appointment with myself, and in this case, with my dog!

When you're in the thick of it or contemplating starting a family and worried about "fitting it all in," start with your calendar.

For me, exercise has always been a huge part of my life, and without it, I don't feel good or like myself. Making sure I stayed physically fit, in the pool and on my yoga mat, was and still is a huge priority for me.

This is how I made sure it happened amidst the intense workdays with three little kids:

1. **START WITH A GOAL:** Mine was "I am going to exercise 5x/week."

2. **MAKE A PLAN AND SCHEDULE IT:** For me, it was Monday, Wednesday, Thursday, Saturday, and Sunday.

3. **BANK THE WEEKEND WORKOUTS:** I made sure Saturday and Sunday, I went for a run ... rain or shine. I had to secure those two days when I had nowhere else to be. If it meant running to or from a kid's game, that's what I did. Or if it meant braving the pouring rain for three miles, I did that, too.

4. **SCHEDULE THE WEEKDAYS STRATEGICALLY:** I chose Monday because it felt like a good way to start the week unless there was an 8:00 a.m. executive meeting, and in that case, I'd trade it for Tuesday. Wednesday and Thursday were set in stone and not to be missed.

5. **PREPARE THE NIGHT BEFORE:** I laid out my clothes the night before and confirmed my commitment before I got into bed. It was non-negotiable when the alarm went off.

6. **CREATE ACCOUNTABILITY:** I let people know—my husband, my assistant, and my teammates—which was my built-in accountability and support system.

This same approach can work for any priority you have, from family dinners to date nights. Don't leave the important things to chance—calendar them.

SET UP SYSTEMS

Three words: **The. Night. Before.** This phrase became our mantra and our strategy to control the chaos as best we could.

When children are young, life requires hyper-organization. If that's your strong suit, more power to you. If it's not, get someone to help you or outsource it. It will save you time, countless headaches, major meltdowns, lost uniforms, missing library books, late arrivals to games or practices, and tons of STRESS. Find a way to create a system so that everything needed on a daily basis has a place that is easily accessible and within reach: coats, shoes, backpacks, lunch bags, practice gear, bags, etc.

I learned some of my favorite hacks from friends whose kids were a little older. One of my favorites was from a good friend with five kids. She only had white socks for her four girls and one boy—for some, they were a little small, and for the youngest, a little big. It didn't matter. She created a big sock drawer and strategically located it right above the shoes and next to the front door. So, when the car was on, and everyone was loading in, there was no last-minute scramble to find the missing sock. (That's a topic for another day, but can anyone solve the lost sock in the dryer mystery? Please!)

SEASONAL ORGANIZATION HACKS

I employed the sock drawer hack for all the seasons:

- WINTER: I transitioned it to a big drawer with bins for hats and gloves.
- SUMMER: It was for sunscreen, sun hats, and sunglasses.

PROJECT PREPAREDNESS

Another big drawer was organized with everything that would be needed for a school project because those time-consuming assignments come often. And when you least expect it, obviously, you're out of glue for the glue gun, and the markers are dry and out of ink!

MEAL PLANNING & SNACK ORGANIZING

We never did a formal meal plan, but we did get the kids involved in preparing the snacks for the week. Just that one simple thing—having them put either Goldfish crackers or pretzels into snack bags for the whole week—was one less tedious step in the morning when Sam was making lunches.

Keep meals simple and healthy *enough* ... a bagel with cream cheese, Goldfish crackers, an Oreo, and apple slices was the go-to lunch, and our kids did just fine in school and got into the colleges of their choice. Don't overthink meals and put too much pressure on yourself. Your worth as a parent is not measured by homemade organic lunches. If you are one of those "make your own baby food" types, good luck—that's all I can say.

TEACHING INDEPENDENCE: KIDS PACK THEMSELVES

As soon as our kids were old enough (around age 6), they packed themselves for all trips. We had only one major mishap when Ashleigh packed clothes for her American Girl Doll for Hawaii, but forgot bathing suits and underwear. We borrowed board shorts and bought underwear at Target—those vacation photos are priceless.

This small act of independence taught responsibility, reduced my mental load, built their confidence, and created natural consequences that became our most cherished family memories.

SETTING SUSTAINABLE BOUNDARIES

Some of the best advice I received from another parent was, "Don't start what you don't intend to continue." For me, this applied to bedtime rituals. With three children, I couldn't commit to an hour-long bedtime with multiple stories per child.

Instead, we all read one story together, and then each child looked at books independently for 15-20 minutes. They could chat afterward if they wanted—Ashleigh often moved to Hank's top bunk after Sam and I left.

This boundary gave quality attention to all three children simultaneously, created a sustainable routine, fostered independence, and preserved evening time for Sam and me. Setting clear boundaries from the beginning saved countless hours of negotiation and prevented the guilt of breaking established patterns later.

SET CLEAR BOUNDARIES FROM THE BEGINNING

Being pregnant gave me permission to say "no" to things that weren't essential. I learned to prioritize ruthlessly, a skill that served me well as both an executive and a mother. When I was at work, I was fully present for my team. When I was home, I was fully present for my family. *Perfect balance doesn't exist, but clear boundaries do.*

YOUR SUPPORT TEAM

Having a network of people to support both you and your family is imperative. Your support system will be your lifeline during the most demanding seasons of balancing career and family.

YOUR PARTNER

I had Sam, who was closer to a saint during these years than anything else I can think of. He handled just about everything at home and with the kids, and consequently, allowed me the freedom to use all of my energy and brain power at my job during the day.

If it wasn't for this, I know I would not have been as successful or effective in my leadership or decision-making. I had the luxury of not having to worry about so many details about the day or the kids, even though I did anyway.

EXTENDED FAMILY AND COMMUNITY

My in-laws were a tremendous source of support. Whether it's your immediate family, your chosen family, your friends, neighbors, or people in the community, this network is critical.

You will need someone to:

- Get a sick kid from school
- Drop off or pick up from practice
- Step in during work emergencies
- Provide backup when plans fall through

Building this support system isn't a sign of weakness—it's strategic preparation for success in all areas of your life.

MINDSET: THIS TOO SHALL PASS

I remember when our kids were first born, and that period of sleepless nights seemed never-ending. A good friend with older kids shared some of the best advice that I still follow and share to this day. She said, "Even though you are knee-deep in this and can't see the light at the end of the tunnel, remember this period will not last forever. You'll come out of it in 8-10 weeks, look back and think, 'Wow, that was tough, but it's over.'" This scenario plays out at every stage of parenthood—if not life itself.

Mindset is one of the most important aspects of managing the natural feeling of guilt as a working mom. No matter how hard you try, how "good" of a mom you are, you will be judged by family, friends, and peers. As Mel Robbins so eloquently and simply says, "Let them." Your mindset is the only thing you can control, and that is what matters.

The reality is you are juggling a lot, doing the best you can, and sometimes you're going to be a superstar mom, and other times you're going to feel like a total failure. And it's OKAY, and it's normal.

When the guilt creeps in, remember:

- Every working parent feels this way sometimes.
- Your children benefit from seeing your ambition and work ethic.
- Quality time matters more than quantity.

- You're teaching your children about balance, perseverance, and following dreams.
- The challenging seasons make the joyful ones even sweeter.

The season of small children is just that—a season. Before I left Nordstrom, when our kids were 4, 6, and 8, every winter for 5 years, we spent 10 consecutive weekends together at the ski mountain in our 36-foot RV. I would often step off the Nordstrom private plane, rush home, swap my designer clothes for leggings, boots, and a beanie, and we'd drive to the mountain.

While other families spent the weekends shuttling between winter sports, sleepovers, and birthday parties, we made a commitment that not only made our kids great skiers, but also bonded us together in a way we couldn't have done at home. We had family ski days, meals on the mountain or in the RV, and hours of sledding and playing in the snow together.

Think about when you take your team on an annual retreat where everyone stays together, eats together, works, and plays together—you build genuine connections.

Those years in the RV were where we formed our strongest family bonds. Sitting at a little table with coloring books and Jenga games, with nowhere to go and nothing to do after 9:00 p.m., we connected deeply.

Looking back now, I can see that what felt like pure chaos was actually laying the foundation for our family's future.

Those early years of marathon days and minimal sleep were an investment that continues to pay dividends in our relationships, our children's independence, and our careers.

There's no perfect formula. The systems and boundaries that worked for our family might look entirely different for yours. The point isn't to copy someone else's blueprint but to be intentional about creating one that honors your priorities and values.

And on those days when you've shown up to work with mismatched shoes or forgotten an important school form, remember to laugh. These moments of imperfection are part of the journey, too, and often make the best stories years later when you're finally enjoying that quiet cup of coffee by the fire.

LESSONS LEARNED

- TRUST IS EVERYTHING—
  I couldn't have maintained my career without completely trusting Sam with our children and home life. Sure, I kept my finger on the pulse, but micromanaging from afar would have been disastrous.

- ORGANIZATION PREVENTS CHAOS—
  The systems we put in place prevented chaos when we were too exhausted to rely on memory or motivation.

- **PERFECTIONISM IS THE ENEMY—**
  The sooner you let go of having the perfect home, perfect meals, or perfect appearance, the happier everyone will be.

- **INDEPENDENCE IS A GIFT—**
  Teaching our children to do things for themselves wasn't just convenient for us; it built their confidence and capability for life.

- **GUILT IS INEVITABLE BUT MANAGEABLE—**
  Every working parent feels guilt. Acknowledging it without letting it control you is the key to mental health.

- **SMALL MOMENTS MATTER—**
  It wasn't the elaborate vacations that built our family bonds but the consistent, small rituals of connection we maintained even in busy seasons.

QUESTIONS FOR REFLECTION

1. What are your non-negotiables that need to be on your calendar every week? How will you protect this time?

   _____
   _____
   _____

2. Which areas of your life could benefit from better systems? What's one system you could implement this week?

_____

_____

_____

3. How aligned are you and your partner on family priorities and division of responsibilities? What conversation do you need to have?

_____

_____

_____

4. What perfectionist tendencies are causing you unnecessary stress? What would happen if you loosened your grip on these standards?

_____

_____

_____

5. Who makes up your support network? Are there gaps you need to fill before adding more to your plate?

_____

_____

_____

6. What boundaries have you established that you're struggling to maintain? Why?

_____

_____

_____

7. How do you currently handle the feeling of guilt? What new mindset might serve you better?

_____

_____

_____

n i n e

WHAT LOVE LOOKS LIKE

*"What you leave behind is not what
is engraved in stone monuments,
but what is woven into the lives of others."*

PERICLES

LESSONS FROM A LIFETIME OF SHOWING UP

MEETING MY FUTURE IN-LAWS

The first time I met my in-laws was at a local bar on the island where Sam and I grew up. Like us, Sam's parents also both grew up on the island, and we all live there still. Christmas night, 1996, brought an epic snowstorm, and the entire city of Seattle, and most especially Mercer Island, was completely shut down for about a week. If it were anywhere on the East Coast or Midwest, the "epicness" would be child's play, literally. But Seattle isn't prepared for these kinds of storms, with upwards of 12 inches in 24 hours. Driving was nearly impossible, certainly not advised. Let's just say we were all snowed in!

So Steve and Colleen, desperate to get out of the house after two or three days of being snowed in, put on their snow clothes and got Sam and his sister's vintage Radio Flyer sled, and with Colleen on top of Steve, they sledded from their home a half mile down the hill to the local bar where they were sitting outside enjoying a pitcher—yes, I said pitcher—of wine. Dressed entirely in their ski clothes, they were the only people sitting outside on the covered porch of the old Roanoke Tavern.

Sam and I, with the same thought process of getting out of the house, somehow navigated the snowy streets of Seattle and drove over to Mercer Island and to the Roanoke to get a beer. Little did we know that the first people we would hear and then see would be his parents. We had just started dating, and we were barely official—not yet to the point of meeting the parents. So this serendipitous introduction was not only funny but also left an indelible impression.

Here they were, high school sweethearts, having met in the fifth grade, now at age 50-something, looking, acting, and sounding like they were newlyweds. I remembered when Sam and I were first hanging out, not even dating, and I asked him why he didn't have a serious girlfriend. He answered, "Until I meet the kind of person where I can have a relationship like my parents do, I don't want to settle." I always remembered that and then, seeing his example firsthand in that moment, I understood the bar he was reaching for (pun intended).

THE FOUNDATION
THEIR RELATIONSHIP WITH EACH OTHER

What struck me most about Steve and Colleen from that very first meeting was how much they enjoyed each other and their genuine connection—they looked at each other with the same spark you'd expect from a couple in the early stages of romance, not one who had been together for over four decades. They sat there bundled up, laughing at each other's jokes, filling each other's glass of wine with not a care in the world. They had made it out of their house, one on top of the other, and there was no place they'd rather be than on that snowy porch at the Roanoke. What's funny is, having known them now for over 25 years, they are always like that. It doesn't matter where they are—their house, our house, their cabin, or at the local pizza parlor. Their relationship doesn't merely exist; it thrives on a steady diet of laughter, love, and genuine enjoyment of each other's company.

Steve and Colleen never lost themselves in just being "mom and dad," like many parents do. They absolutely loved their kids, but they knew their marriage needed attention, too. They'd tell us stories about family trips where they'd hand Sam and his sister KC some spending money and shoo them off for a while so they could have "alone time." They were diligent about protecting their time together. It wasn't selfish; it was the best gift they could give their kids—parents who genuinely enjoyed each other's company.

Sam grew up observing what a real partnership looks like. He picked up on the unwritten rule they lived by—that putting their marriage first actually made them better parents, not worse ones. Their solid relationship gave him a foundation of security that shaped who he became. While raising our own kids, we follow the same pattern. We protect our time as a couple, knowing that when we're good, the kids feel it, too. It's a ripple effect of stability that flows from our relationship out to everyone else in our family.

FRIENDS FIRST

Our relationship with Steve and Colleen started when we were dating, mostly on Friday nights at their house for happy hour after work at their house. Before long, it became a ritual I looked forward to all week and was always initiated by us. We'd call after work, asking what they were doing, and they invited us over. They'd welcome us into their home, uncork a bottle of wine (for us, they drank box wine at that time!), and create this cozy space where conversation flowed as freely as the wine. We talked about our days, our jobs, and things like recipes or summer plans. There was never an interrogation about our relationship or subtle probing about our future plans—just genuine interest in who we were becoming together.

I remember sitting on the hearth in their living room as Colleen passed simple appetizers while Steve told stories about his job at Shell Oil. He would describe his day and the conversations with the gas station owners in his region about the pricing plans for the upcoming weekend. I was fascinated by the dynamics of supply and demand and the prices of oil that dictated our local price per gallon. Steve was a natural-born leader, and I loved hearing how he negotiated and worked with the people in his orbit to maximize sales and profit.

Colleen, on the other hand, would often pull out an old family photo album to share pictures and stories of their family camping trips to Europe. They literally packed and brought sleeping bags, tents and the other supplies necessary to camp in the mountains in Austria! I'm pretty sure this scared me a little (I am not really a camper), but it always solidified how grounded and unique they were. It struck me then how much I was learning about them as people, not just as "Sam's parents." Their careers, their travels, their priorities and values, and their different personalities—it all unfolded naturally over glasses of cheap Chardonnay and laughter. They were showing us, rather than telling us, what partnership looked like.

HOW SUPPORT SHOWS UP

When we decided to get married in Puerto Vallarta, Mexico, their support shifted from casual to crucial. On the day of our wedding, while most of our guests were enjoying the beach and pre-ceremony cocktails, Steve and Colleen were trudging through the humid streets of town with us. I remember Colleen wiping the sweat off her neck as she helped me translate the final payment details with the wedding planner, while Steve negotiated with our driver in his broken Spanish. They could have easily said, "You've got this," or "Can't your wedding coordinator take care of this?" but that wasn't their style. They came with us, sweated it out, and never once made us feel like we were imposing on their vacation.

That pattern continued when we bought our first house—the one we still call home today. We borrowed a large portion of the down payment from them to buy the house in the first place. Once we were the proud owners, they appeared at our doorstep with painting clothes already stained from previous projects, ready to transform our yellow walls into something that felt like us. Steve, whom we quickly nicknamed MacGyver, somehow knew exactly how to patch the mysterious hole we discovered behind the refrigerator, while Colleen helped me organize our kitchen with a logic I still benefit from today and decorate with her style and flair.

But it was when Declan was born that their support became not just helpful but essential. They were the first ones at the hospital, bringing not just gifts for the baby but practical wisdom we didn't even know we needed then for the rest of our lives. Colleen, ever the saver, gave us a curated book of newspaper clippings, articles, cartoons, and anything else you can imagine with parenting advice. She had saved all of these snippets since Sam was born and organized them into a book for us by life stage. That book has had a permanent spot on our bookshelf in our living room and has become a reference guide more than we ever imagined.

I still laugh thinking about that first day home from the hospital with Declan. Sam had run to the store for some supplies, and I found myself alone with this tiny human who suddenly needed a diaper change. Panic rising in my throat, I called Colleen.

"Hi Colleen, what are you doing right now?" I asked, trying to sound casual while Declan wailed in the background.

"Just lighting a fire, about to pour a glass of wine," she replied, the picture of relaxation.

"Do you need something?" she asked, hearing something in my voice I was trying to hide.

"Actually, yes," I admitted. "I need some help with Declan's diaper."

To this day, I can't explain why changing that first diaper alone felt so overwhelming. But within minutes, Colleen was at our door, still wearing her house slippers, ready for duty. She didn't take over completely or make me feel incompetent— she just stood beside me, offering quiet guidance and an extra pair of hands. When Sam returned home, he found us all laughing on the couch, the momentary crisis forgotten.

That's the thing about Steve and Colleen's support—it never arrives with conditions or leaves you feeling indebted. It simply shows up when needed, adjusts to what's actually helpful rather than what they think should be helpful, and then recedes when the moment has passed.

> THEIR HELP NEVER ARRIVED WITH CONDITIONS OR LEFT YOU FEELING INDEBTED. IT SIMPLY SHOWED UP WHEN NEEDED.

What I've come to appreciate most is how this support system has created a sense of abundance for our children. They don't just have two adults wholly committed to their wellbeing—they have four. The "bigger source of love, support, and safety net" that Steve and Colleen provide hasn't made our role as parents less significant; it's made our family more resilient.

In a culture that often glorifies independence to a fault, Steve and Colleen's willingness to be leaned on has been transformative for our family. Their support comes without the invisible strings I've witnessed in other family dynamics—no subtle expectations of eternal gratitude, no keeping score, no judgment about our parenting choices or lifestyle decisions.

CREATING FAMILY TRADITIONS

The Fourth of July at Steve and Colleen's cabin became our favorite days of the summer, if not the entire year. They'd go to their cabin a week early, prepping everything from themed bunk room pillows to homemade potato salad and flags throughout the house, inside and out. They would build an enormous float to sit on the top of their boat trailer for all of the grandkids to ride in during the local parade! With fresh crab ready, s'mores supplies packed, and more Pop-Tart flavors than you can imagine, they handled every detail so we could just show up, relax, and have fun together. This wasn't just throwing a party—this was Steve and Colleen building memories brick by brick. The amount of work they put in was crazy, but you'd never hear a word about how tired they were or what it took. They just wanted us all to have a great time.

Similarly, Christmas morning had its own special tradition. They'd park in our driveway, but before ringing the doorbell, they'd quietly stack five gift boxes on our porch—one for each grandchild. Each box had the exact same number of presents (they kept a strict count), all thoughtfully chosen for each kid. Every box came with a massive stocking stuffed with treasures from the Five and Dime, thrift stores, or later, Amazon finds. Nothing fancy or expensive, just small things wrapped with care. It wasn't about the gifts themselves, but the message they sent: "I love you, I know you, and I picked this just for you."

These traditions might seem silly or over the top to outsiders, but I've watched how they've woven our family together over the years. The children anticipated these gatherings well in advance, not just for the celebration itself but for the sense of continuity they provided. In a world that changes at dizzying speeds, these traditions offered our kids the gift of something reliable, something that connects their past to their present and future.

What Steve and Colleen understand implicitly—without ever needing to read a parenting book—is that these traditions are the glue that holds families together. They're creating this shared story that all of us are part of, these touchpoints we come back to year after year. They're not just letting memories happen by chance. They're deliberately building them—it is like they're making deposits into this family bank that keeps growing in value as the years pass. It's their way of saying, "This is who we are. This is what matters to us."

BEING PRESENT IN THE HARD TIMES

The true measure of support isn't how it shows up during celebrations, but how it manifests during challenges. Never was this more apparent than when I experienced postpartum depression a few weeks after I had Ashleigh, our third child.

WHAT LOVE LOOKS LIKE

I remember that morning so vividly—I couldn't get out of bed, something that had never happened to me before. I called my best friend Jill, who talked me through the simple act of putting my feet on the floor and walking downstairs. In Sam's office, I desperately searched for information on "Brooke Shields postpartum depression," having recently read she'd gone public with her struggles. When I scanned the article listing symptoms, my heart raced, seeing myself in nearly every description. *"This is me—now what do I do?"*

The symptoms weren't comprehensive, but the ones I had were overwhelming and debilitating. I learned quickly that postpartum depression doesn't discriminate—it doesn't matter how strong, energetic, focused, or capable you usually are. It can appear without warning, leaving you feeling like a stranger in your own life.

With Sam away on a golf trip for a couple more days, I called Steve and Colleen. I didn't have to explain much—something in my voice must have told them everything they needed to know. Steve's response was immediate and unwavering: "Come here. Now. We've got you." His comforting, loving, and supportive encouragement gave me the strength to pack up the baby, get into the car, and drive the two hours to their cabin, where they were babysitting our other two kids, Declan and Hank.

What followed were days of the most tender, loving care imaginable. Colleen took the baby for long stretches so I could sleep. Steve made sure I ate regular meals. They tag teamed caring for our older children with seamless effort. They created a cocoon of safety around me, never once making me feel weak or inadequate for struggling.

They didn't try to "fix" me with platitudes or dismiss what I was going through. Instead, they simply surrounded me with practical support and unwavering acceptance. In those dark days, they became more than in-laws or even parents—they became my safety net, letting me heal without judgment or impatience.

THE GRANDPARENT EFFECT

From the moment our kids entered the world, Steve and Colleen jumped into grandparenting with both feet. They didn't just want to be occasional figures who showed up with presents at Christmas and birthdays—they wanted real relationships with each grandchild.

They'd show up at our door ready for anything, never saying no when we asked for help. When the kids were tiny, they were changing diapers, warming bottles, and cleaning up messes with no complaints. I remember thinking how thankless it must have felt some days—babies aren't exactly great at showing appreciation—but they were making these incredible deposits into relationships that would pay dividends years later.

The way they connected with the kids was so intentional. Colleen would take Declan out to her garden, her little hands barely big enough to hold the trowel she bought her. They'd come back muddy and happy, and before long, she was teaching me about which plants needed sun versus shade.

A regular outing with all of the kids was to the local thrift store—Colleen's passion for a good bargain became their first lessons in value-seeking and smart shopping.

Steve, with his endless patience, would spend hours in his workshop with them. I can still picture the kids standing on footstools to reach the workbench, learning to pound nails without hitting their thumbs (mostly), and building wobbly but treasured creations. "Look what Grandpa helped me make!" became a regular announcement in our house.

But beyond these fun moments, they were teaching our kids values that have stuck. The way Steve meticulously maintained everything from the dishwasher to the lawn mower instead of replacing them. How Colleen would clip coupons, bargain hunt, and stretch a dollar further than anyone I've ever known. The kids absorbed these lessons about money, saving, and living below your means just by being around them.

We made sure to never take this gift for granted. Even though they lived literally two minutes up the street (I timed it once during an emergency cookie dough situation), we insisted on proper hellos and goodbyes, on please and thank yous. "It's a privilege to have grandparents who want to be in your life," we'd remind the kids. Not in a stern way, but as a simple truth.

Now, we get the payoff of all those years. Our college kids will call them while walking across campus, not because we've nagged them to check in, but because they genuinely want to talk to Grandma and Grandpa. They share real stuff with them—their classes, their friends, their worries. These aren't awkward obligation calls. They're actual conversations between people who really know and like each other. Our kids don't see Steve and Colleen as just "the grandparents"—they're people who've shown up at soccer games in the pouring rain, who knew their favorite breakfast before they could even speak, who've been steady fixtures in all the moments that mattered, big and small.

LESSONS LEARNED & THE PATH FORWARD

What have I learned from watching Steve and Colleen over these 25+ years? The most profound lesson is that strong families don't happen by accident—they're built through thousands of intentional choices made over decades. Their consistent presence in our lives offers a blueprint not just for in-laws, parenting, or grandparenting but for creating a community of support that sustains its members through life's inevitable challenges.

What's amazing about Steve and Colleen's approach is how giving fills them up rather than drains them. They pour themselves into our family—driving carpool when kids were little, showing up at games, babysitting at a moment's notice—without ever keeping tabs or making us feel indebted.

Instead of depleting them, this generosity has created this amazing circle of care where everyone feels supported. They never expect anything back for all they do, but ironically, that's exactly why they get so much in return. Their reward is having grandkids who want to call them from college, who seek out their advice, and who genuinely like spending time with them. It's like they figured out this secret that most people miss—the more freely you give support, the richer your relationships become.

For those without built-in family support, their example points to the importance of creating chosen family through friends and your community. Finding ways to volunteer, join faith communities, or participate in activities that build meaningful connections can generate the same kind of support network that has been so valuable to us.

The multi-generational legacy Steve and Colleen are creating extends far beyond their immediate influence. The patterns they've established—prioritizing their relationship

> IT'S LIKE THEY FIGURED OUT THIS SECRET THAT MOST PEOPLE MISS— THE MORE FREELY YOU GIVE SUPPORT, THE RICHER YOUR RELATIONSHIPS BECOME.

while still being incredible parents, offering unconditional support, creating meaningful traditions, showing up consistently in good and hard times, and building individual relationships with grandchildren—are being absorbed by our children, who will likely carry these values into their own future families.

I've come to see that the most valuable inheritance they're passing down isn't material—it's a template for how to truly connect with others. Their example shows that the effort invested in relationships yields returns that money simply cannot buy: the security of knowing you belong to something larger than yourself, the comfort of having people who show up without being asked, and the joy of traditions that anchor your place in time.

LESSONS LEARNED

- PRIORITIZE YOUR PARTNERSHIP—
  Steve and Colleen never disappeared into just being parents. Their thriving relationship created a foundation of security for all of us. Sam and I follow this pattern—when we're good as a couple, that stability flows to our children.

- BE FRIENDS FIRST—
  Those Friday happy hours showed me how they welcomed us as friends, not just "Sam's parents." They created space for genuine connection

without interrogating our relationship, showing rather than telling what partnership looks like.

- **OFFER UNCONDITIONAL SUPPORT—** Their support arrives without conditions and never leaves us feeling indebted. It simply shows up, adapts to what's actually helpful, then steps back. Our children benefit from having four adults wholly committed to their well-being instead of just two.

- **CREATE INTENTIONAL TRADITIONS—** Steve and Colleen understood that traditions weave families together. Fourth of July at their cabin, Christmas morning gift boxes—they weren't just letting memories happen by chance. They were deliberately building our family story, making deposits that grow in value with time.

- **SHOW UP IN HARD TIMES—** During my postpartum depression, Steve's immediate response—"Come here. Now. We've got you"—became my lifeline. They didn't try to "fix" me with platitudes but surrounded me with practical support and acceptance when I needed it most.

- **BUILD INDIVIDUAL RELATIONSHIPS—** They formed unique connections with each grandchild through gardens, workshops, and countless small moments. Now our adult kids call them not from obligation, but because they genuinely want to share their lives with grandparents who've always shown up.

- **GIVE WITHOUT KEEPING SCORE—**
  Their generosity fills them up rather than drains them. They've discovered a secret—the more freely you give support without tallying returns, the richer your relationships become.

- **LIVE WHAT YOU VALUE—**
  Our kids absorbed crucial lessons just by watching them—Steve's meticulous maintenance instead of replacement, Colleen's legendary ability to stretch a dollar. These values took root without a single lecture.

- **CREATE A LEGACY BEYOND MATERIAL WEALTH—**
  Their greatest inheritance isn't financial—it's this template for authentic connection. The security of belonging to something larger than yourself can't be bought.

- **STRONG FAMILIES ARE BUILT INTENTIONALLY—**
  Watching them for 25+ years taught me that strong families don't happen by accident. They're built through thousands of small, consistent choices that create a community capable of sustaining its members through life's inevitable challenges.

QUESTIONS FOR REFLECTION

1. What examples of healthy relationships did you witness growing up? How have these shaped your expectations and approach to your own relationships?

   _____

   _____

   _____

2. In what ways do you prioritize your primary relationship while still being present for others who need you?

   _____

   _____

   _____

3. How do you offer support to those you love? Is your support conditional or freely given?

   _____

   _____

   _____

4. What family traditions are you cultivating that will create lasting memories and a sense of belonging?

   _____

   _____

   _____

5. When faced with others' difficult times, do you step in with practical help or step back with well-meaning advice? What would change if you approached these moments differently?

   _____

   _____

   _____

6. How might you create or strengthen your "chosen family" if biological family support isn't available to you?

   _____

   _____

   _____

7. What values are you modeling that you hope the next generation will absorb and carry forward?

_____

_____

_____

BALANCE IS BULLSHIT

THE TRUE MEASURE OF
SUPPORT ISN'T HOW
IT SHOWS UP DURING
CELEBRATIONS, BUT
HOW IT MANIFESTS
DURING CHALLENGES.

ten

STRONG DOESN'T MEAN INVINCIBLE

"What I thought I was going through was a natural part of becoming a mother. I had no idea that I could feel so lost, so dark, and so completely out of control."

BROOKE SHIELDS

A POSTPARTUM STORY FROM THE OUTSIDE LANE

I gripped the steering wheel, knuckles white, fighting back tears as I drove home with my three children. The oldest was four, the youngest just days old. I was a successful executive and a confident mother of three, known for my resilience and optimism. Yet in that moment, I wasn't sure I could make it the last few miles home. This wasn't just the "baby blues" or normal postpartum adjustment—this was something darker, something I hadn't experienced with my first two children, something I never expected to face.

Everyone tells you that having a baby changes everything. They talk about the sleepless nights, the hormonal shifts, and the way your body transforms. What they don't tell you is how postpartum depression can strike even the strongest among us, how it doesn't care about your previous successes or your natural optimism. I learned this the hard way after my third child was born when a perfect storm of physical complications and hormonal changes brought me to my knees.

The Mayo Clinic lists several symptoms for people experiencing the "baby blues": mood swings, anxiety, sadness, irritability, feeling overwhelmed, crying, reduced concentration, problems with appetite, and trouble sleeping. I experienced a few of these symptoms when Declan and Hank were born, as most mothers do. Overwhelmed for sure—I remember looking at Declan in that moment after she was born when the nurses clean the baby and then hand them to you skin-to-skin for that initial bonding moment. I remember so vividly saying to myself, "Oh my God, how am I going to do this? I don't know if I'll be able to take care of a baby." I just felt like crying. I handed her back to Sam while I caught my breath, and as Sam has been since that moment, he was calm, quietly confident, and managed not to show his level of overwhelm. He was my rock in those first few precious and vulnerable minutes.

When Hank was born, knowing what to expect, all of the moments before, during, and after his birth were predictable and manageable. But things were very different with Ashleigh.

I had an epidural with the prior two deliveries, but this one took an unexpected turn. The attending anesthesiologist had trouble locating the injection point and had to make at least three attempts before administering the anesthesia. What I didn't know at the time was that he had inadvertently punctured a pin-sized hole in my spinal cord—not noticeable until your head is completely upright and your brain detects something is really wrong as you're leaking spinal fluid.

After delivering Ashleigh, while I didn't feel great, I didn't feel particularly bad until I had to get up out of bed for that dreaded first walk to the bathroom. I practically fainted and asked to go back to bed immediately. When we were ready to be discharged, excited to return home with our third bundle of joy, I could barely tolerate sitting in the wheelchair from the hospital room to the curbside. My head felt like it was going to explode.

At home, I immediately went to my bed, trying to find some comfort lying flat. That first night home, breastfeeding Ashleigh while Sam managed four-year-old Declan and two-year-old Hank, is one I will never forget. Neighbors wanted to come over to meet Baby Ashleigh, and I remember hearing Sam say to them on the phone, "I know she'd love to see you, but she's not doing very well. This is really different than with the other two kids. I'll keep you posted."

Serendipitously, that same neighbor checked in late that evening and happened to have some pain medication from a recent surgery. Sam was in close contact with my OB-GYN, who gave us the okay to take something to relieve my pain. The pain in my head that night was so excruciating—I thought my head was in a vice. I was in and out of a pain-induced sleep while trying to feed my precious little baby.

First thing in the morning, we found ourselves in the ER, where we finally discovered the source of my excruciating pain. The doctor explained they would perform what's called a "blood patch," a procedure where they would use my own blood to seal the hole in my spine. They sent us home afterward, assuring us I would turn the corner. But medical certainties have a way of unraveling in the dark hours, and that's exactly what happened to me. Despite the pain medication prescribed by my OB-GYN, I could barely make it through the three-hour window between doses. The patch had failed. Forty-eight hours after delivering Ashleigh, we were back in the ER, this time with real fear coursing through us. After a CT scan and another spinal examination, they discovered the hole was larger than initially thought, requiring another patch. I lay on the gurney, my newborn daughter beside me for feeding and comfort, my voice breaking as I pleaded with the doctor for relief. Through my pain-blurred vision, I caught sight of the doctor's name tag and recognized him from St. Monica's, our local church. As if sensing my recognition, he bent down, placed a gentle hand on my shoulder, and said, "I know who you are—I'm friends with your parents at the church. You're in my care now. I will take great care of you." In that moment, his words were as powerful as any medicine, transforming a sterile hospital room into a place of familiar comfort.

It took weeks to recover—six shots in my back, not to mention the normal recovery after delivering a baby. The hole in my spinal column took time to heal, and the headaches required Tylenol with codeine for almost eight weeks.

In the midst of my physical recovery, I still wasn't feeling like myself. My normal positive attitude and optimistic outlook just weren't there. I felt flat. I remember going to the grocery store with Sam and saying, "I'll just stay here in the car while you go in." I had no energy to even get out of the car. And when he was in the store, I would start crying. For no reason. I would try to wipe away the tears before he returned because I felt ashamed. "Why on earth was I crying?" I was getting better, we were home together, Ashleigh was the best baby, and Hank and Declan were adjusting. But I just was ... not myself.

Then came Sam's planned three-day golf trip. He had arranged for his parents to take Declan and Hank to their cabin, and I would be home with Ashleigh on my own. That sounded like a great plan until night one. I woke up to feed her and then had the most terrifying feeling I can ever remember. I could not stop crying; I was alone, and I didn't know what to do. Sam was in an area without cell coverage or Wi-Fi. I called my niece in NYC, and she stayed on the phone with me for a couple of hours.

In the morning, I called my best friend Jill, who became my lifeline. She talked me through getting out of my bed and downstairs in our house. That's when I went to Sam's office and searched for "Brooke Shields postpartum depression." She had just shared publicly about her struggles with postpartum depression. When I scanned the article and came across her list of symptoms, I thought, "This is me—now what do I do?"

> I DIDN'T HAVE EVERY SYMPTOM OF POSTPARTUM DEPRESSION, BUT THE ONES I HAD WERE OVERWHELMING AND DEBILITATING.

I didn't have every symptom of postpartum depression, but the ones I had were overwhelming and debilitating. I know it's different for every woman, and it doesn't matter how strong, energetic, focused, loving, kind, or amazing you are. Postpartum depression is a real condition that can show up unexpectedly after giving birth, and it's an incredibly difficult condition to push through.

Jill stayed on the phone with me while I did the most mundane of tasks. "Change into some sweats, and call me back when you do. Call me when you and Ashleigh get into your car. Call me after you go to the Starbucks drive-through. Call me after you call your father-in-law." If I didn't have her holding my hand that day, I'm not sure how I would have managed those simple things.

I returned home with a coffee and called my OB-GYN to share what was happening. He offered some suggestions, including a prescription for anti-depressants to help control my hormones. I didn't get that filled, wanting to try a few other strategies first.

My neighbor Dave knocked on the door to check on the new baby, and I shared with him how I was feeling. Unknown to me, he had battled mental health issues for much of his life. He said, "I know how active you are—I've seen you running for years. I think you need to get your endorphins going again. Even a long walk might really help you." He was so right. So much of feeling like myself was tied to being active and healthy, and I was neither of those things. I took his advice and began to resume some physical activity.

I called Sam's parents and updated them. I knew if Sam couldn't get home for another day, I needed to be with his parents and my other kids. His dad's comforting, loving, and supportive encouragement gave me the courage I needed to get into the car and drive two hours to be with them. I was in the most tender, loving care imaginable with them.

After two days, it was time to head back home. The terror I felt at the idea of getting behind the wheel with all three kids under four years old was almost debilitating. I had to dig deep into that grit and resilience I'd learned from as early as I can remember. This was by far one of the hardest things I had done as an adult. I gripped the wheel, played the songs the kids liked, and held back the tears until I took the exit to Mercer Island. I drove into the driveway, where Sam was waiting for us, and I just wept. I wasn't out of the woods, but I was so much better than I had been two nights ago when I left him a dozen desperate messages.

Looking back, I realize how naive I had been about postpartum depression. If you had asked me about it before, honestly, even though I would have been sympathetic to any woman experiencing these symptoms, I would have believed that a positive outlook and healthy lifestyle were preventative. I wrestled with myself, feeling like I should be able to "snap out of it." After all, I was a high-achieving executive, a proven mother, super healthy with a positive outlook, and determined to find my footing and get back to our normal family life. But postpartum depression doesn't care about any of that. It's a real medical condition that requires support, understanding, and sometimes professional intervention.

LESSONS LEARNED

- STRENGTH COMES IN MANY FORMS— My experience taught me that true strength is not about powering through alone—it is about knowing when to reach out for help. Sometimes, the strongest thing we can do is admit we're struggling and accept support from others.

- **BUILD YOUR SUPPORT NETWORK EARLY—**
  The people who helped me through—Sam, Jill, my niece, Dave, and my in-laws—weren't just casual acquaintances. They were people I had invested in relationships with over time. Those relationships became my lifeline when I needed them most.

- **LISTEN TO YOUR BODY AND MIND—**
  Physical and mental health are deeply interconnected. Dave's suggestion to get moving again wasn't just about exercise—it was about reconnecting with a part of myself that made me feel whole.

- **CHALLENGE YOUR ASSUMPTIONS—**
  I had to confront my own biases about mental health and postpartum depression. Success, stability, and strength in other areas of life did'nt make me immune to postpartum depression.

- **SMALL STEPS MATTER—**
  Recovery didn't happen all at once. It was built on small actions—getting dressed, making a phone call, taking a walk. Each tiny step forward helped create momentum toward healing.

QUESTIONS FOR REFLECTION

UNDERSTANDING SUPPORT SYSTEMS

1. Who are the people in your life you could call at 2 AM if you needed help?

   _____

   _____

2. What holds you back from reaching out when you're struggling?

   _____

   _____

3. How can you strengthen your support network before you need it?

   _____

   _____

EXAMINING PERSONAL BELIEFS

1. What assumptions do you hold about mental health challenges?

   _____

   _____

2. How might these beliefs affect your response if you or someone you love experiences similar struggles?

3. What does being "strong" mean to you, and how has that definition evolved over time?

PREPARING FOR CHALLENGES

1. What strategies do you have in place for managing difficult times?

2. How do you recognize when you need help?

3. What activities help you feel most like yourself?

CREATING CHANGE

1. How can you help reduce the stigma around postpartum depression and mental health?

   _____

   _____

2. What would you tell someone else going through a similar experience?

   _____

   _____

3. How can you be a better support person for others facing these challenges?

   _____

   _____

MOVING FORWARD

Remember that everyone's journey with postpartum depression is different. What worked for me may not work for everyone, but the fundamental lessons remain: you are not alone, you are not weak, and there is no shame in seeking help. If you recognize any of these symptoms in yourself or someone you love, reach out to a healthcare provider. The earlier you seek support, the better equipped you'll be to navigate this challenge.

Your strength isn't measured by how well you handle everything on your own, but by your courage to face challenges honestly and accept help when you need it. Sometimes, the bravest thing we can do is admit we can't do it alone—and that's not just okay, it's human.

STRENGTH ISN'T MEASURED BY HOW WELL WE HANDLE EVERYTHING ON OUR OWN ... SOMETIMES, THE BRAVEST THING WE CAN DO IS ADMIT WE CAN'T DO IT ALONE.

eleven

SAM'S CASE FOR THE STAY-AT-HOME DAD

"For others, it's laziness. You're too lazy to work and support your children. I'm talkin' about men! You call yourself 'Mr. Mom'—God calls you a bum! St. Paul says you are worse than an infidel. Let me look you right in the eye and tell you that Hell is your future home if all you do is sit on your backside and let your wife support you."

REVEREND JOHN HAGEE

OPENING STATEMENT

When Loretta assigned me a chapter in her book, my first thought was, *No problem — this will be easy.* I kept a journal when the kids were young and actually wrote quite a few stories about my experience, so I knew my memories would be iron-clad. Then I started thinking about how to summarize 13 years of being home with the kids into one relatively short chapter. And my second thought was, *shit, this is gonna be hard.*

You can read the story of how we arrived at this decision in Chapter Six, "Trading Places," but when Loretta and I decided that I would stay home with the first baby (at that time, gender and name TBD), I never imagined it would continue as long as it did, nor that I would be as fulfilled after having done it. I was excited about the decision, but I was not ecstatic about the nomenclature for what I had chosen to become: "Stay-at-home Dad," "Mr. Mom," or the worst, "House-Husband," they all sounded too politically correct and feminine (not to mention heavy on the hyphens). And though I never questioned our plan to reverse roles, this chapter's opening quote from the good Reverend Hagee did echo a societal sentiment for us infidels.

By the time Declan was born in 2001, I had been a trial lawyer for nearly 10 years and a prosecuting attorney handling criminal cases for about 4 years. I was young and energetic, and I loved my job. I was trying more serious cases and had no intention of leaving that position permanently. My first murder trial was underway when Loretta went into labor with Declan. I'll never forget sleeping on a recliner chair in our hospital room those first couple of nights (we milked that hospital stay), then rushing down to the courthouse in the morning to cross-examine defense witnesses. I brought actual photos of Declan to stare at while we were on breaks or while a witness was droning on unresponsively to my questions.

A week later, the jury convicted, and the trial was finished. And though I did not know it at the time, so was my career as a lawyer.

WHY WOULD ANY GUY DO THIS?

"You are so lucky — I would do that in a second!" I heard this phrase nearly unanimously from working dads upon learning that I was the one home with our three young kids. Their certainty was only more confirmed when they learned that Loretta was the one working full-time and paying for everything. I always understood the allure of lying around eating Bonbons and watching Oprah or ESPN, but I was also skeptical. You see, I knew a ton of women with high-paying, big-responsibility careers, but I saw none of their husbands lining up to stay home. There are obviously many reasons why couples continue to work, why they decide one will stay home, and why that one is almost always the wife. I'm not here to second-guess or judge those decisions. But if you're a couple considering the path less traveled, I might have a perspective and some advice worth consideration.

To begin, accepting a new definition of myself and my role was challenging. As one can imagine, there were countless Nordstrom work dinners, social events, and other events where I would meet new people, often couples. Inevitably, someone (usually the working husband) whom I just met would ask me, "What do you do?" In the beginning, when I had reduced to working only 2 days per week, I would answer this way: "I work part-time as a prosecutor, but mostly I'm staying home with our baby, and Loretta is the worker." As I settled into the role and stopped working part-time several years later, however, I embraced the new definition and would typically answer, "I stay home with our kids." And that always brought the same reply about how the other guy would have done that in a second, and then usually, he was no longer interested in chatting.

One conversation has always stuck with me. When our kids were very young, my friend, "Todd," stayed home from his corporate job to, as he put it, "be the mom" because his wife was out of town for a couple of days. They had two kids around the same ages as our two youngest at the time (7 and 5). He was ribbing me, jokingly saying how tough it was to be home with the kids. He then said (more sincerely) that he couldn't believe his wife actually complains about being home with the kids. He bragged he was getting a ton done, having fun with the kids, there was no stress, and it was all so very relaxing and fun. I agreed and told him I used to have the same feeling when I worked for a whole day. I loved the freedom from not doing the kid stuff; I got to get up in the morning and just get myself ready to go, no lunches, no homework check, no refereeing, no finding socks and forcing them on, no outfit changes or heavier coat arguments. I loved the mental challenge of the work, the adult time, and, of course, the money. I told him I couldn't believe anyone actually complains about working full time while their spouse takes care of the kids, the house, the chores, the errands, and the planning.

His response: "Touché."

WHY DID I THINK I COULD HANDLE IT?

I suppose there were three reasons I felt confident in the decision to stay home with the baby and then to continue to stay home as we kept popping out kids. First, even though I don't believe I had ever changed a diaper before Declan, for a few years while I was in elementary school, my mom basically ran a daycare out of our house for working moms in our community. So every morning, there were anywhere from 3-5 toddlers being dropped off before I left for school. I must have picked up a thing or two through osmosis, or at least gained the confidence that I could actually handle it. And as I got a little older, I started babysitting to earn money so I could buy all the things my parents could not or would not buy for me.

The second reason I felt comfortable with sacrificing my career goals was that I watched my dad do that throughout my entire childhood. My dad worked for Shell Oil Company from the time he graduated from college until he ultimately retired. As a kid, I remember many discussions about my dad being offered promotions contingent upon his moving to Houston, Texas. He was not a fan of Houston and thus turned down offer after offer of more money, more prestige, and a pathway up the ladder. He chose to keep the family where we were and decided we would make do with what he could make and save. Every night, he was home by 5:30 at the latest, helped with my and my sister's homework, helped coach many of our sports teams, and attended all of our games. Those lessons were impactful because my dad was modeling a philosophy that prioritized family over career. So, even though I had never considered being a stay-at-home dad, I knew I could handle it, and I was confident it was the right decision.

The third reason was that I was confident in my masculinity and wasn't concerned about the potential for feeling emasculated. It's a valid concern, but it only takes root if one lets it take root. I never did, so it was never a problem for me or for us as a couple.

Shortly thereafter, I knew I had made the right decision when Declan was 20 months old, and Hank was only 2 weeks old. I was sitting at the dining room table, on the phone (crooked in my neck). I was holding Hank in my left hand while feeding him a bottle with that hand. My right hand was simultaneously putting a diaper on Declan's doll in response to her demand for an immediate diaper change for "baby Sally." All while dealing with something work-related on the phone call. Who says guys can't multitask?

Loretta and I agree that I was probably the better choice to be home with the kids when they were little. I'm better at dealing with emergencies, I'm patient, and I'm far better at hanging out at home, playing games, watching movies, and enjoying downtime with the kids. And unlike her, I read the small print, which is a metaphor for how we live our lives a little differently from each other. This became clear when Declan was around 20 months old. I found a small box of dog treats in the kitchen cupboard. The thing was, we did not own a dog. Loretta had purchased these "cookies" and had been feeding them to Declan daily for about a week. They were undeniably dog treats. Now, in Loretta's defense, the box was about the same size and very similarly logoed as those animal cracker cookies: A bright yellow box with a cartoon bus on it with a bunch of animals riding in the bus. On the other hand, the box also says "The Barking Bus," and "You Better Believe It's a Dog Biscuit," and "Dog Treats" all over it. And if that weren't enough, she had to buy it in the pet section of the grocery store.

So perhaps it wasn't all the babysitting and lessons from my parents, but rather, I was the safest choice of the two of us to stay home!

WHAT WAS IT LIKE TO BE HOME WITH 3 KIDS IN A ROLE-REVERSED MARRIAGE?

Once Declan was born, my career trajectory obviously veered off path. Gone were crime scenes and cross-examinations, guns, and gangs. Instead, dirty diapers, mom's groups, and isolation at the park became my new reality. I traded adrenaline for monotony, intellectual challenges, and adult interaction for play dates and Teletubbies — those infernal Teletubbies. In return, I got more than I ever expected: happy, well-adjusted kids and an inspiring marriage.

So what was it like? Summarizing the day-to-day experience would be impossible in one chapter, but I kept quite an extensive journal and actually wrote many stories with an eye toward a book someday. I've chosen several of those stories that illustrate many of the aspects of a role-reversed marriage, and that capture the issues about division of labor, discipline, and sociological stigmas and double standards attached to being a stay-at-home dad.

The stories are included in full in the appendix at the end of this book, but here are some teaser summaries:

- *The Night I Learned I Didn't "Do" Enough*: This one is a great example of the best way to passive-aggressively win an argument with your wife over why the house wasn't clean when she got home from work. [see appendix, page 315]

- *The Great Grape Standoff*: Fortunately, Loretta was out of town, so I could go head-to-head with a stubborn three-year-old boy staging a hunger strike in opposition to eating two green grapes. I'm pretty sure the statute of limitations has long expired for the child neglect charges. [see appendix, page 322]

- *Teacher Appreciation Week*: With three small kids and tons of teachers, these annual weeks were brutal. Fortunately, stay-at-home dads are largely given a pass, but the pressure is still there because if I screw up, it makes Loretta look bad. Unfortunately, this teacher appreciation week preceded my daughter's birthday week, and let's just say I forgot something critical. [see appendix, page 330]

- *Jesus, Mary & Joseph*: Good manners are the key to raising good kids. Please and thank you. Clearing their dishes. Standing up when adults enter the room. Eye contact. Oh, yeah, and not saying "fuck." [see appendix, page 336]

- *Bloody Thursday*: What's the old saying about being thrown to the lions? That pretty much captures the drive to my daughter's annual doctor appointment the moment I realized I'd never heard whether Loretta actually made good on her promise to discuss menstruation with Declan. Let's just say I did as good of a job as any dad could do explaining how blood was gonna start coming out of his 11-year-old's vagina any day now. *Just typing that sentence was a challenge*—now imagine having to deliver that news! [see appendix, page 339]

LOOKING BACK, WHAT WERE THE PLUSES AND MINUSES?
FOR ME, FOR US, FOR THE KIDS

Like any role, job, or major undertaking, there are pluses and minuses. Aspects of the job you love, and some you dread, or some that simply frustrate you. Here are some of both ...

PLUS

When the kids were little, I knew everything about them. Certainly more than Loretta did, simply because I was there all day with them. I knew Declan liked to color in the letter "o" whenever she wrote a word containing that letter. I knew she needed to express herself by dressing herself—and boy, did she come up with some combinations that Loretta would never have allowed. I knew Hank's favorite lines from the movie *The Incredibles*. I knew he was easily frustrated if he didn't pick up a new skill quickly, whether in school or sports. And I knew Ashleigh loved to sing before she did. She was also the most stubborn and the only one who required a lock on the outside of her door, so I didn't have to stand there holding the door during her time-outs. As they got older and became teenagers, that level of understanding helped me parent each of them differently, and I'd like to think, more effectively. My working dad friends simply didn't have that opportunity because they were never able to spend the time.

SAM'S CASE FOR THE STAY-AT-HOME DAD

MINUS

The tedium. When the kids are young, the work of staying home isn't difficult; it's just tedious, repetitive, and semi-thankless. When people would say things to me like, "You have the tough job" (as compared to my wife), they don't truly mean it. I know this because I've never heard anyone heap praise onto a nanny for doing the same job. Similarly, most nannies don't aspire to a long career of nannying. It's an interim job at best for most. I'll never forget our part-time nanny joking that it was okay for her to act young because she "was doing the job of a twenty-year-old girl" (our nanny was 25 at the time). I pointed out, with mock offense, that she was actually doing the work of a 35-year-old man (my age at the time).

PLUS

Even the kids can see it. When Ashleigh was around 6, she got up on a Friday morning and thought it was Saturday. She came downstairs in her pajamas for breakfast, and I asked her why she wasn't dressed for school, and she said, "Because it's Saturday." To which I responded, "Sorry, honey, but today is Friday, so go back up there and get dressed quick." To that, she responded in an impressively snarky tone, "Every day is Saturday for you," as she slunked back upstairs to change. She was right, however. Every day is basically a Saturday.

MINUS

You're a lone soldier out there in a sea of women, many of whom see you differently. Some look at you suspiciously when you're at the park as if you're there looking to kidnap some kid. That seems more plausible to them than the fact that you're the primary caregiver. Or, husbands feel weird about you going over to their home while they're at work to have a play date with the kids.

PLUS

Having the luxury of time with your kids and in your home is a privilege. While your wife is at a high-powered, important meeting, you're washing the remnants of mini pancakes off plastic plates and actually tearing up over some story on the Today Show about a woman who delivered two stillborn babies and then finally, she and her husband had their own child after their nurse offered to be a surrogate for them. How different your days are from your wife's and how different they are from the way they used to be. But how excellent, if not a little syrupy.

MINUS

I wish my kids could have seen me try a criminal case. They've seen me lecture at the University of Washington Law School about trying criminal cases, but that's not exactly the same thing.

PLUS

There is a double standard that benefits stay-at-home dads. In short, we are not judged the same way on every little thing, whether it's how we look, what we're wearing, what our kids are wearing, what we bring to the potluck or school event, or how we discipline our children in public. Watching moms not discipline their bratty kids used to drive me crazy. But then I realized why I was in a different position. The moms worried about how they appeared to the other moms. I wasn't worried about that for two reasons. First, I simply didn't care what they thought. But, second, I also enjoyed the double standard to my benefit: I was a dad actually at the park with my kids, and that was more than they could say about their husbands. Those moms were more likely to silently judge Loretta, who abandoned the family for her career. Moms judging moms is a thing. Stay-at-home dads fly under the radar.

MINUS & PLUS

The grass might often look greener—but it's green on both sides. Although I would not change a thing about our decision to reverse roles, and let's be honest, I probably got the better straw in picking my role. But if the positions were reversed and I was able to be a prosecutor and mimic Loretta's earning path, I would have been happy to continue working while she stayed home with the kids. There wouldn't have been a peep of a complaint from me in that situation. And this is no knock on Loretta; it's more of an example of how men and women are different with respect to sociological expectations. Women are the last line of defense with the kids because society still expects the woman to stay home and be the primary caregiver. So when a woman elects to work, she feels the judgment and carries the guilt of being the parent who abdicated their role. Men, on the other hand, simply don't feel this way. Fortunately, we each understood and appreciated the sacrifices the other was making for the team.

And the team thrived.

I REST MY CASE

I can pinpoint the day I knew this whole stay-at-home dad thing was going to work out. It was January 13th, 2007. It was on that day that I changed history.

Hank (3 years old) had just gone pee in our bathroom, and Declan (5 years old) came into the bathroom after him to pee. She put the seat down and looked up at me, and said, "Daddy, why do boys never put the seat down after they go pee so girls can go next?" I was stunned. I was being given the chance to do something that almost never occurs in nature— the chance to disabuse a woman about whose responsibility it is to put the toilet seat up or down. Since the dawn of time, girls have been asking this question to their mothers, and their mothers have brainwashed them into thinking it's the boy's responsibility. I looked down at my precious daughter and asked, "Why is it Hank's job to put the seat down? What if a boy wants to pee after you go pee and you've left the seat down? Why should he have to put it up? Is that fair?"

She had no answer. And though that felt like a victory, if you think I don't put the seat down, you haven't read this book very closely and clearly have not met Loretta.

So that's it in one big nutshell. All this could be your life's trajectory, too. Would you really do it in a second? The clock is ticking.

LESSONS LEARNED

WITH RESPECT TO CHILDCARE AND HOUSEHOLD DUTIES—

- **LEARN HOW TO COOK. IF YOU CAN READ, YOU CAN COOK—**
  You need to notice when you're about to run out of stuff to eat—this stuff is also called "groceries." To get them, you'll need to go to what stay-at-home moms call the "grocery store." You've been there before, just not for everything. And when you get home, you have to put it all away. Where it goes.

- **EMBRACE CLEANING. THE TIDIER YOUR HOUSE IS, THE MORE PEACEFUL YOUR LIFE WILL BE—**
  If things are working right, the home should oscillate between a train wreck and something

more Zen. You will be criticized for not picking up enough. Don't worry about the critics; they aren't those generally responsible for doing it all day long.

- **DON'T GET ONE OF THOSE MOM-LOOKING DIAPER BAGS—**
Get something that is more on-brand for a guy.

- **IF YOU HAVE MORE THAN TWO KIDS, GET A MINIVAN—**
Now, I know you think chicks don't dig guys in minivans, but ... okay, well, you're probably right on that one—BUT, they are so user-friendly, and that makes your life easier. I drive a Ford F150 now, but I do sometimes miss that minivan.

- **CREATE ROUTINES FOR THE MORNING—**
Create routines for the evening.
Don't sweat the days.

- **DON'T TELL A CHILD WHAT YOU PUT IN THEIR LUNCH—**
It's not a negotiation, and they will not starve if they elect to eat none of it.

- **FIGURE OUT A WAY INTO THE "MOMMY MAFIA"—**
The Mommy Mafia is the powerful and all-knowing cabal of stay-at-home moms in your community.

They have this job down to a science. They are wary of you but also curious and willing to help.

And the most important rule:

- **NEVER *EVER*, UNDER *ANY* CIRCUMSTANCE, MAKE A THREAT YOU DO NOT INTEND TO CARRY OUT—**
  If you say, "If you do this, then this will be the consequence," you better mean it. If your kids do not believe the "then" will happen if they violate the "if," you have lost the power struggle, you've lost the war, and you will raise brats. Worse still, brats who don't respect you.

WITH RESPECT TO YOUR MARITAL RELATIONSHIP—

- **QUEEN-SIZED BED—**
  First, the forced proximity ultimately encourages physicality. Second, it's too small for children to sleep with you—which, again, encourages physicality. Third, it's easier to make the bed (and if you make the bed rather than expecting your wife to make the bed, this encourages physicality).

- **SLEEP NAKED—**
  See above.

- **NO TV IN THE BEDROOM—**
  Do I really need to spell this one out for you, too? We broke this rule about 5 years ago, and I've regretted it ever since.

- **PRIORITIZE YOUR WIFE—**
  Make sure to prioritize your relationship with your wife by getting away for a night or two here whenever possible. It's very easy to be overwhelmed by the business of life, kids, and work, so it requires at least one of you to be proactive about alone time.

WITH RESPECT TO YOUR OWN SANITY—

- **DO SOMETHING RELATED TO YOUR CHOSEN PROFESSION, OR AT LEAST SOMETHING YOU ENJOY—**
  Make sure it requires the use of your brain and/or your brain and your hands. Preferably, something you would also be getting paid to do. It could be teaching, working part-time in your field, coaching, or mentoring. It could be art. It could be any product or service that you control and are paid for.

- **GET IN SHAPE—**
  You have time. You're not a runner? No one is. To borrow a catchphrase, *just do it.*

QUESTIONS FOR REFLECTION

1. Is caregiver role reversal an option within your relationship?

   _____

   _____

   _____

2. If you're dating and considering getting married, have you discussed how childcare would work? If you are married but have not started your family yet, have you discussed how childcare would work?

   _____

   _____

   _____

3. Are you capable of making a career sacrifice for the family, and does it make sense to your shared goals and priorities?

   _____

   _____

   _____

4. Will your wife promise not to use her financial leverage as a club to beat you with?

   _____

   _____

   _____

5. Projecting forward, what will you be most proud of: your career's success or your family's success?

   _____

   _____

   _____

6. It's only emasculating if you let it—are you man enough to take the risk?

   _____

   _____

   _____

t w e l v e

A BOSS, A BITCH, OR A BOLD BRAVE LEADER?

> *"In the future, there will be no female leaders. There will just be leaders."*
> SHERYL SANDBERG

You might find it ironic that I was raised by a stay-at-home mom who never had a credit card, never wrote a check, and never had her own bank account. My dad would leave checks made out to the grocery store, the gas station, the paper boy, and the milkman in advance of his sometimes-three-week global travel for his job. If my mom wanted anything extra, she would have to underspend the amount written on the check and squirrel away a few dollars to buy whatever else she had her eye on.

But when I think about how I became a leader—and what shaped me early on—I think of my mom. My dad traveled a lot for work, so by default, she was our team leader. She got all five of us to and from school, to practices, tennis tournaments, and swim meets. She was our biggest cheerleader and fiercest supporter. She taught us how to treat people, live with compassion and empathy, and show respect. She also taught us how to get along with each other—and how to master the ultimate team dynamic: a family of seven.

Too often, we disregard the leadership lessons right in front of us. My mom wasn't just a great mother—she was a masterclass in leadership. She maximized a small budget into outsized ROI and embodied the perfect player/coach balance: diving into details when needed while empowering us to learn from our mistakes. She was the kind of leader I later sought out professionally and aspired to become—someone who demanded excellence but created space for growth and learning.

What I learned from my mom is that you don't need a fancy title or big P&L responsibility to be a true leader. It's about being genuinely human while balancing compassion with high expectations. My mom showed me that leaders can be gracious, kind, and humble while still setting standards, enforcing consequences, and building confidence in others. She wasn't "charismatic" by traditional definitions, but her consistent example

A BOSS, A BITCH, OR A BOLD, BRAVE LEADER

and clear values successfully mobilized our family more effectively than any fire-and-brimstone approach ever could.

So here's the question I want you to consider as we dig deeper into this subject: What kind of leader do you really want to be? I am not asking what kind of leader society expects based on your gender, background, or position—but what kind of leader do YOU want to be?

WHAT KIND OF LEADER DO **YOU** REALLY WANT TO BE?

I've spent decades navigating the complexities of leadership as a woman in corporate America. I've been called a boss (sometimes with admiration, sometimes not), I've been called a bitch (almost never with admiration), and I've worked hard to become what I consider a bold, brave leader. Along the way, I've learned that while leadership doesn't care about your gender, almost everyone else does.

This chapter isn't about complaining about unfair standards or lamenting challenges. It's about acknowledging the reality of the leadership landscape and giving you tools to navigate it successfully, regardless of your gender or leadership level. I do this because the world needs more leaders who can combine strength with empathy, confidence with humility, and boldness with wisdom.

THE BOARDROOM COLLECTION

There was a section of my wardrobe that you could either call the "boardroom collection" or the "funeral collection"—take your pick. When I was front row at fashion shows, visiting showrooms during market week, or attending new store openings, I would wear the latest fashions. But I also had a dedicated collection of pencil skirts, tailored pants, and dark blazers strictly reserved for executive committee meetings, board presentations, or investor calls. These comprised my boardroom collection.

It wasn't about style—it was about credibility. No matter the trends of the season, there was a visual uniform I was expected to wear when addressing the most powerful rooms. And while I was leading the women's division of the company, I couldn't help but wonder—did my male counterpart, also a senior executive, have a "boardroom" section in his closet?

Spoiler alert: He didn't.

In fact, I'll never forget him showing up for back-to-back meetings in the exact same suit, having flown cross-country in it, complete with wrinkles and a faint coffee stain on his shirt. He gave his presentation. Nobody blinked.

Can you imagine the reaction if I had done the same in the female equivalent? Let's not even go there.

I had to think not just twice, but three or four times, about every outfit. The neckline. The heel height. The skirt length. Then, multiply that by ten when I was representing the brand in the market or at fashion week. The pressure wasn't just to be professional—it was to be polished, stylish, and flawless always. Brilliant *and* beautiful. Competent *and* couture.

So, rather than wasting precious energy on this every quarter, I got strategic. I created my "boardroom collection"—a no-brainer capsule wardrobe that turned this double standard into my secret weapon. Here's what I've learned: every person has obstacles that nobody else faces.

You can either play the hand you're dealt—or learn to stack the deck. The magic happens when you turn challenges into your superpower. While my male counterparts blended together in their navy suits, I used my wardrobe to reflect different dimensions of my leadership.

One of my favorite examples? At the Flagship store, on one of the busiest days of the year. I wore a bright pink blazer. It wasn't random—it was intentional. Pink is professional, it's memorable, and it naturally puts people at ease. That day, we needed calm and confidence. I showed up in both.

It was never about dressing to impress. It was about showing up ready to lead—meeting the moment with energy, clarity, and purpose. And focusing on what really mattered: serving the customer and driving results.

FROM CAREFUL TO CONFIDENT

The leadership landscape has always been riddled with double standards. When men lead with strength, presence, and assertiveness, they're celebrated as decisive and commanding. Women displaying these same traits are often labeled aggressive, difficult, or abrasive. It's not just perception—it's a reality that shapes our professional journeys.

During my time as an executive at Nordstrom, one of my senior male counterparts would offer his unfiltered opinion in leadership meetings without hesitation, barely raising his hand before blurting out, "No way, that's ridiculous!" or "Come on, that's an impossible idea!" He did this unapologetically, and nobody batted an eye. If I had behaved the same way, especially as a young female executive, I would have been harshly criticized, if not asked to leave the room.

I, in contrast, would wait to be invited to share my opinion and would carefully frame my comments: "These are all interesting approaches, but I think the best solution for the business and our company culture would be X, Y, or Z." Our communication styles were opposites, partly due to personality, but largely because of the unwritten rules governing how men and women are expected to behave in leadership settings.

Over time, I found my voice in those leadership meetings. I began speaking before being called on, respectfully but directly voicing my opinions and concerns and proposing alternatives without apologies or qualifications. I never raised my voice, but rather, I spoke more slowly and deliberately, following the mantras that "less is more" and "it's not what you say but how you say it." This approach earned me far more respect than I ever imagined possible.

There's an instinct to copy other people's communication styles because you can see it modeled. But it's important to remember that's THEIR recipe for success, not yours. What matters is finding your unique, authentic voice that feels like you, so that you never have to feel like you're pretending to be someone you're not. The energy it takes to maintain anything that is not authentically you will rob you of the creativity and resourcefulness needed to be successful.

Do the work of finding your sweet spot. When you're at your best, how do you feel comfortable responding to conflict? How do you motivate teams? How can you lead someone who's failing to a path of success? How do you show up as the fiercest competitor that you are while bringing the team along for the ride?

> FIND YOUR UNIQUE, AUTHENTIC VOICE SO THAT YOU NEVER HAVE TO FEEL LIKE YOU'RE PRETENDING TO BE SOMEONE YOU'RE NOT.

MAKING THE HARD CALLS WITHOUT LOSING YOUR SOUL

Navigating business cycles at a publicly traded company presents both predictable and unprecedented challenges. As an executive managing a $2B P&L, organizational restructuring—aka eliminating jobs in the name of cost-cutting—was by far the most gut-wrenching aspect.

My male colleagues would methodically work through eliminations as casually as deleting files on their computer—no emotion displayed. I saw each name as a person with a family, an identity, and a livelihood at stake. Men were praised as "level-headed" for their detachment, while I walked a tightrope between being labeled "emotional" or "cold."

When I took time to consider different perspectives and adjust decisions, I was labeled a "flip-flopper"—the same thoughtful consideration my male counterparts received praise for as "strategic thinking."

Is it fair? No, of course not. But it's reality, and it's not worth selling your soul over it.

DECISION-MAKING FRAMEWORK

I developed an approach that helped me be both strategic and humane. I would craft scenarios A, B, and C—both near-term and long-term—without attaching names initially. I focused first on business needs, desired outcomes, and necessary skills and capabilities before evaluating specific people.

By thinking a couple of steps ahead, I could anticipate when someone might face multiple disruptions. If I knew that an individual would face a demotion or job change more than once, I could make a more strategic and compassionate decision, ensuring they only went through disruption once rather than repeatedly. Ultimately, if I did have to take someone out of their job, I did my best to ensure dignified exits. The most surprising outcome? Often, the people I had to let go would end up hugging me and expressing gratitude as they left my office—confirmation that treating people with respect during difficult transitions matters more than they'd ever know.

The irony wasn't lost on me that my human-centered approach ultimately created better business outcomes than the systematic, detached method considered more "professional." What had been framed as a potential weakness became my greatest strength. The challenge wasn't choosing between empathy and efficiency—it was finding the courage to integrate both when others tried to tell me they were mutually exclusive.

WHY YOU DON'T WANT TO BE A "BOSS"

There's nothing more demoralizing than being on the receiving end of a directive.

When I was a national buyer, the leadership team brought in consultants—none of whom had ever bought or sold merchandise—to develop and implement a sweeping transformation strategy. Input was gathered exclusively from those consultants, while the people closest to the business—the buyers—were completely ignored.

The result? A master plan created in isolation, with radical, top-down decisions and zero collaboration. Buying teams were expected to execute without input or context. Vendor budgets and assortment plans were handed down with no transparency, stripping us of any creativity or ownership. No surprise—the initiative completely failed.

It failed because it ignored our core business model: the inverted pyramid. In this model, the pyramid is turned upside down, where the customer sits at the top—because the customer is the most important—followed by the salespeople, then buyers and managers, with the executive team and CEO at the bottom. Ideally, ideas and initiatives originate with the frontline—those closest to the customer—and are then supported and refined by leadership. This experiment completely disregarded that structure.

That experience left a lasting impression:

- Involve the people closest to the work.
- Explain the "why" behind decisions.
- Don't expect blind execution—invite contribution.

Real leadership isn't about control—it's about creating the kind of environment where people can think clearly, stay focused, and do their best work. A boss has a title; a leader earns trust. A boss gives orders; a leader inspires action. A boss manages tasks; a leader sets the standard through how they show up, what they expect, and how they treat people.

A BOSS HAS A TITLE—A LEADER EARNS TRUST.

ADAPTING YOUR LEADERSHIP STYLE

Great leaders know it isn't one-size-fits-all. Leadership is situational, and effectiveness requires flexibility. Whether you're managing a diverse team, parenting different kids, or moving from a fashion show to a boardroom, success depends on your ability to read the room and adapt your approach.

You won't get it right every time—and that's okay. I've learned to evolve as I go, staying aware of what's needed in the moment and adjusting without losing who I am. Over time, credibility isn't built by sticking to one fixed style—it's built by delivering results, earning trust, and staying grounded in your values, no matter the setting.

Style-flexing is a learned skill—usually through plenty of trial and error ... and more error.

Here are a few techniques I've developed over the years:

- **BECOME A SHARP OBSERVER.** Before key meetings, I paid attention to how the most respected voices in the room communicated—their pace, tone, level of detail, and body language. It wasn't about copying them, but about understanding what worked in that environment—whether that meant being data-driven or leaning into storytelling.

- **USE SITUATIONAL PERSONAS.** I have a "boardroom version," a "team meeting version," and a "one-on-one version." They're all authentically me, but I emphasize different things depending on the moment. It's like picking the right outfit for the right occasion. Same person, different presentation.

- **ADJUST YOUR DELIVERY.** In high-stakes settings, I speak more deliberately, trim the fluff, and drop the qualifiers. When I'm coaching a team, I slow down, ask more questions, and explain my thought process. With external partners, I match their style and meet them where they are.

- **SIGNAL THE SHIFT.** When I need to switch gears—especially with a collaborative team—I call it out: "I'm going to be direct here because we're up against a timeline." That small shift builds trust and prevents whiplash.

- **MATCH THE ROOM'S ENERGY, THEN GUIDE IT.** If a meeting starts tense or intense, I begin with the same tone, then gradually bring it down. It's far more effective than trying to counter the energy right out of the gate.

Flexing isn't about shrinking—it's about being intentional so your leadership lands in the right way, with the right people, at the right time.

THE SOCRATIC METHOD OF TEACHING

I had a woman on my team—let's call her Sally—who was one of the most pleasant people I worked with. But as her responsibilities grew, she began to struggle. Unlike my other direct reports, who could handle weekly sign-off meetings with ease, Sally needed a different approach.

She'd show up with neatly organized papers and color-coded spreadsheets, expecting a quick approval. Instead, I asked questions she couldn't fully answer. Rather than signing off on incomplete work or telling her what to do, I'd send her back to find the answers and return in a few days.

This happened three times. By round three, something shifted. She returned with deeper knowledge, stronger analysis, and she started anticipating the questions before I asked them.

It would've been faster to just fix her work—but teaching her how to think differently and investing in her development paid off. She went on to win a performance award that year, and I'll never forget the pride I felt handing her that bonus. That moment confirmed what I already believed: leadership isn't about making your job easier—it's about helping others reach their full potential.

> **LEADERSHIP ISN'T ABOUT MAKING YOUR JOB EASIER—IT'S ABOUT HELPING OTHERS REACH THEIR FULL POTENTIAL.**

It's the classic "teach them to fish" philosophy. I want people to solve problems confidently, even when I'm not in the room.

Critical thinking became the cornerstone of my leadership style. I challenged my team with tough questions and helped them build their own process for decision-making. If someone left my team more capable—strategically, operationally, and as a leader—then I'd done my job.

LEADERS EMERGE FROM THE LEAST EXPECTED PLACES

One of my favorite examples of bold, brave leadership came from a woman I'll call Michelle—a 24-year-old junior account executive at Elie Tahari. At a time when the Nordstrom business was struggling, she pitched an idea to both me and Elie himself: create an exclusive, lower-priced collection to reinvigorate the brand.

Most people at her level wouldn't have dared to propose something so bold, but she did.

In a high-stakes meeting with my senior leaders and the executive team from Tahari, I turned to her and asked, "Why do you think this will work?" The room went silent.

Michelle laid out her idea with clarity and confidence—and everyone listened.

That moment didn't just change how others saw her—it changed how she saw herself.

Leadership doesn't require a title. Sometimes, it's simply about being prepared, having a point of view, and being brave enough to speak up.

Together, we grew the business from $3 million to $30 million annually. Michelle remains a close friend, and we continue to mentor each other.

QUALITIES OF EFFECTIVE LEADERSHIP

Over the years, I've seen a clear difference between "coaching" and "directing" as leadership styles. Coaching—teaching, developing, and encouraging—builds long-term capability and trust. Directing—ordering, enforcing, challenging—might drive short-term results, but rarely inspires loyalty or growth.

I always aimed to protect my team while holding them to high standards. When our business was underperforming, and pressure from the executive team was intense, I made a conscious decision not to let that stress roll downhill. Instead of relaying the pressure or panic to my team, I chose to absorb it—to stand in front of them, shield them from distraction, and give them clarity and confidence to do their jobs.

I knew that if they felt the full weight of what I was carrying, it would shake their focus. They didn't need to feel the fear. They needed to feel direction. That moment taught me a valuable truth: great leaders don't amplify pressure—they filter it so their teams can stay grounded, motivated, and productive.

FINDING YOUR LEADERSHIP BALANCE

Finding your leadership style isn't about picking one extreme or the other—it's about finding that sweet spot where you lead with strength, stay grounded in who you are, and never misuse the power that comes with the role.

STRENGTH WITHOUT AGGRESSION

- You can be assertive but not obnoxious.
- You can be aggressive but not an asshole.
- You can be confident but not cocky.

EMPATHY WITHOUT WEAKNESS

- You can be humble but not a martyr.
- You can be likable but not a pleaser.
- You can be organized but not controlling.

RESULTS WITHOUT RUTHLESSNESS

- You can be independent but not selfish.
- You can be strategic and still collaborative.
- You can be decisive without being dismissive.

DIRECTION WITH RESPECT

- You can be direct without being disrespectful.
- You can be firm on standards without being inflexible.
- You can be results-focused without sacrificing relationships.
- You can be driven without being difficult.

Forget trying to strike the "perfect balance" of traits—like being 50% assertive and 50% warm. That equation doesn't exist. Just like in life, leadership requires you to lean in fully to what's needed in the moment. Some days, that's grace. Other days, it's grit.

It's not about balance—it's about alignment. With yourself, your values, and what the moment truly demands.

NAVIGATING FEEDBACK AND THE LIKABILITY TRAP

Over the years, I was sometimes told I was "too direct" or "too tough," while men showing the same behaviors were praised as "strong" or "decisive."

Instead of spending energy getting frustrated by every double standard, I came up with a simple system:

1. Take the emotion out of it.
2. Look for the valid insight.
3. Reframe the feedback in neutral terms.
4. Decide if it's worth acting on.

Likeability still matters—especially for women—but that doesn't mean softening who you are. I've found that setting clear boundaries early earns respect without losing warmth. When I need to assert myself, I stay professionally direct. Phrases like "I see it differently" signal confidence without crossing the line.

You can be direct without being disliked, respected without being feared, and warm with-

YOU CAN BE DIRECT WITHOUT BEING DISLIKED, RESPECTED WITHOUT BEING FEARED, AND WARM WITHOUT BEING WALKED OVER.

out being walked over. The goal isn't to walk a tightrope—it's to show up with intention.

LEARN TO TOOT YOUR OWN HORN

If you've ever stumbled over how to talk about your own success, you're not alone. I've watched plenty of smart, capable women underplay their accomplishments—while their male peers say, "I led," "I achieved," or "I delivered" without hesitation.

I used to do it too—until I realized how we talk about our work directly shapes how it's valued. Over time, I found ways to advocate for myself clearly and confidently without losing the collaborative tone I value. It's not about grabbing credit—it's about not giving it away.

SHIFTS THAT MADE A BIG DIFFERENCE

- Instead of "I'm proud of what I did," say, "Under my leadership, the women's division increased profitability by $90M and grew top-line revenue by over $500M."

- Instead of "I'm pretty good at ..." say, "The knowledge and insights I've gained over three decades make me well equipped to take on these challenges."

- When someone gives praise, don't deflect. Simply say, "Thank you—I worked hard on that."

ONE FINAL TIP

- Frame accomplishments as updates. Saying, "I wanted to share some progress on our key initiatives ..." is a natural way to highlight results without sounding like you're bragging.

These small language shifts helped my work get noticed—without ever compromising my leadership style: clear, collaborative, and direct.

YOUR LEADERSHIP LEGACY

Throughout this chapter, I've shared what I've learned about leading as a woman—from finding your voice in tough rooms to making hard calls with empathy to advocating for yourself without apologizing for it. The journey to becoming a bold, brave leader isn't about perfection—it's about consistency, growth, and staying true to your values. These strategies have helped me hone my leadership style:

FLEX YOUR STYLE WITHOUT LOSING YOURSELF.

The leadership playbook wasn't written with women in mind, but that doesn't mean we have to play a different game. I learned how to flex depending on the room—more direct in board meetings and more nurturing when building trust in high-pressure environments. It's not about changing who you are—it's about adjusting how you show up without ever compromising your values.

CREATE PATHWAYS FOR OTHER WOMEN.

When I joined my first corporate board, I didn't just say we needed more women—I came with names, resumes, and a business case. I've mentored countless women not just with advice, but with access. The pipeline doesn't build itself. If you've made it through the door, hold it open behind you—on purpose.

CHANGE THE SYSTEM BY SUCCEEDING ON YOUR OWN TERMS.

I didn't wait for permission to lead differently. When a people-first approach to restructuring reduced disruption and improved performance, I made the case with data. Results speak louder than resisting something, and they empower you to change what leadership looks like.

LET GO OF THE MYTH OF BALANCE.

Leadership—like life—isn't about splitting everything evenly. It's not about perfect time blocks or color-coded calendars. Balance is bullshit. What matters is alignment: knowing what you value and showing up accordingly. Women are expected to lead with strength but not too much, show emotion but never too deeply. The pressure to "balance" it all is paralyzing. The truth is: real leadership is messy. Some days I led from the front. Other days, I cleaned up the mess in the back. The goal isn't balance—it's choosing the right response for the right moment. And that's where the power lives.

Your title or resume won't define your leadership legacy, but by how you lead, how you make people feel, and what you make possible for others. The world doesn't need more women trying to lead like men. It needs women who are bold enough to lead like themselves.

So, as you think about what kind of leader you want to be—boss, bitch, or bold and brave—remember: leadership is a choice we make every day in how we show up, how we treat people, and what we stand for.

WHAT KIND OF LEADER WILL YOU CHOOSE TO BE?

Just don't waste your energy trying to balance it all perfectly. That myth keeps too many women small. Lead fully. Live fully. Let go of balance—and go all in on becoming who you're meant to be.

LESSONS LEARNED

- **AUTHENTIC LEADERSHIP TRANSCENDS GENDER—**
  While society may have different expectations based on gender, true leadership comes from being genuine while adapting your approach to different situations.

- **EMPATHY AND EFFICIENCY ARE NOT MUTUALLY EXCLUSIVE—** My most successful business outcomes came from approaching decisions with both strategic thinking and genuine concern for people.

- **LEADERSHIP DEVELOPMENT REQUIRES INVESTMENT—** Taking time to develop critical thinking in others might seem slower at first, but it creates stronger, more capable teams in the long run.

- **POWER AND COMPASSION CAN COEXIST—** You don't need to choose between being respected and being liked—the most effective leaders find ways to be both.

- **YOUR LEADERSHIP STYLE IS YOURS TO DEFINE—** Despite pressures to conform to others' expectations, I found my greatest success by integrating my authentic self into my leadership approach.

QUESTIONS FOR REFLECTION

1. What leadership qualities do you naturally embody, and which ones do you need to develop more intentionally?

___

2. Think about a time when you felt pressured to lead in a way that didn't feel authentic. How did you navigate that situation, and what would you do differently now?

___

3. How do you currently balance being direct with being respectful in challenging conversations? Is there room for growth in either direction?

___

4. In what situations do you find it most difficult to adapt your leadership style? What might be holding you back?

   _____

   _____

   _____

5. Consider your own "boardroom collection" of behaviors or presentations. What aspects of yourself do you feel you need to modify in certain settings, and are those adjustments serving you well?

   _____

   _____

   _____

6. How do you currently talk about your accomplishments? Practice reframing three recent achievements using the more direct language discussed in this chapter.

   _____

   _____

   _____

7. When faced with making difficult decisions that affect others, what process do you follow? How might you incorporate both strategic thinking and empathy into that process?

_____

_____

_____

8. What will be your leadership legacy? What do you want others to say about how you led and the impact you made?

_____

_____

_____

thirteen

MENTORS MATTER

*"We make a living by what we get,
but we make a life by what we give."*

WINSTON CHURCHILL

I was a newly appointed executive at Nordstrom and the youngest in company history. I was charged with overseeing and transforming the largest and most underperforming division in the company with a responsibility of just under $1.5B. A little less than three months into my new role, I was asked to present my turnaround plan not only to the board of directors, which was comprised of CEOs from multiple Fortune 500 companies, but also to the top financial analysts from Wall Street. My turnaround plan and impending positive results for the women's division would largely impact the stock performance of the company. Needless to say, the pressure was intense, and the arena was completely foreign to me.

As a total rookie, scared and naïve, I turned to my friend and senior colleague, Jack, for some sound advice. At about 6:30 a.m., the morning of my presentation, I called him. "I'm sorry to call so early," I said, shaky but determined, "but I have to present to the board and the analysts in an hour and a half, and I'm paralyzed with fear. I know I have a good plan in place, but what if they grill me, and I don't have all the answers?"

Still finishing his first cup of coffee, he reminded me as he had once before, "You've got this. There is a reason they put you in this job. You know what to do and have a solid plan in place. Just share that with conviction, and don't be afraid to tell them you don't have all the answers yet."

He calmed me down and instilled confidence in me, and I did just as he said. I went into that boardroom with a sense of calm and self-assurance, and I shared my plan to turn around and rebuild the business.

That early morning call to Jack changed everything—not just the presentation, but how I've approached every challenge since—with a sense of composure and the conviction that I was the right person for the job. It wasn't a sophisticated strategy—just straightforward advice about being myself and communicating clearly and honestly.

The truth? I had never considered Jack as my "mentor." But rather a colleague I could call in a moment of need. But that's precisely the point about mentorship that I've come to understand: it rarely announces itself with formal titles and scheduled meetings. Instead, it appears in unexpected moments of connection, when wisdom flows naturally between people who care enough to be present for each other.

WHEN THE TEACHER BECOMES THE STUDENT

A few years ago, I was invited to be a guest lecturer at Columbia Business School and the McCombs School of Business at the University of Texas. I expected to share my perspectives and proven frameworks on brand building and go-to-market strategies, but both professors surprised me by asking for something different. They wanted me to talk about my professional journey, my life, and the role mentorship had played along the way.

I was so excited by this shift in focus—it gave me a chance to connect with these bright, ambitious students on a much deeper, more personal level. During both sessions, I found myself sharing stories about the mentors who had shaped my career and influenced my life decisions. The students' questions were thoughtful and insightful, digging deeper into how these relationships had guided my path.

As I watched their faces light up with interest and curiosity, I could tell I had their undivided attention—something rare in students these days. I had an "aha" moment—one that became a catalyst for this book. These students weren't just craving classic business principles and frameworks; they wanted real-life perspectives and inspiration. They were looking for something more—stories that reflected the messy, unpredictable, and rewarding journey of building a career and, more importantly, a life you love.

For years, my husband, Sam, had been encouraging me to share more of my story. "You need to tell more people," he would say. "Find a way to scale your experiences so you can inspire and mentor more people." I'd heard him, but standing there in front of those students, I felt it. Their energy, their interest, and their hunger for something real reinforced what Sam had been telling me all along.

And in that moment of dialogue and Q&A, where I was supposed to be teaching them, but they were unknowingly teaching me, I was reminded that mentorship is rarely a one-way street. It flows in multiple directions. Sam was mentoring me on the direction of this book. I was mentoring the students about career development and life. And those same students were mentoring me through their reactions, questions, and eagerness to learn.

MENTORSHIP IS RARELY A ONE-WAY STREET. IT FLOWS IN MULTIPLE DIRECTIONS.

This organic, back-and-forth exchange of wisdom is what mentorship is all about—and it's exactly what I want to capture in this chapter. The truth is, every single person has something to teach and something to learn, no matter where they are in life or their career.

WHAT IS A MENTOR?

If you think about it, we're all shaped by the people we meet along the way—those who offer advice, challenge our thinking, or simply help us see things a little differently. Some of these people become our mentors, often without even realizing it.

Over the years, I've had mentors guide me through major life decisions, help me handle tragedy, navigate the ups and downs of parenthood, and even help me make sense of entrepreneurship—just to name a few. But my mentors weren't just formal advisors. They were people I knew, some better than others, who acted as guides, walking alongside me through different stages of life. They offered support, perspective, and sometimes a gentle push in the right direction.

What's funny is that one of my greatest mentors doesn't even know she is my mentor. She's never given me formal advice, never sat me down for a career talk, and has no idea how profoundly she's shaped my thinking. That's because mentorship happens in unexpected ways and with unexpected people—if we're willing to pay attention.

Mentors can be formal or informal, long-term or situational, and they often come from the most unexpected places. A mentor doesn't have to be someone older or more experienced in every aspect of life. In fact, some of the most profound mentorships can come from children who offer pure, unfiltered wisdom, friends who see things from a different angle, or even strangers whose insights strike a chord at just the right moment.

A LESSON FROM HANK
FINDING RESILIENCE IN SIMPLICITY

I remember a moment when my son taught me an unexpected lesson about resilience. It was after being unexpectedly fired from Nordstrom. I was left feeling embarrassed, confused, and scared. One afternoon, while driving Hank to basketball practice, he sensed that something was off. From the backseat, in his sweet, matter-of-fact way, he simply said, "Don't worry, Mommy. There's always a happy ending."

His innocent words were profound, and they stopped me in my tracks. In that moment, I was reminded that resilience and strength often come from the simplest, most unexpected places. That quiet reassurance from my son gave me the perspective I needed to stay calm and trust that things would eventually fall into place. Moments like that reinforce that mentorship isn't always about formal relationships—it's about being open to learning from anyone, anywhere.

PERSONAL BOARD OF ADVISORS

When I think about my mentors, I don't just think of formal relationships. My mentors include a diverse mix of people—my husband, our kids, the students I interact with, my swim teammates, authors whose books inspire me, podcast hosts who challenge my thinking, business colleagues, and close friends. These are the trusted voices I turn to for insight, ideas, and thought partnership across a variety of topics—my go-tos when I'm making big decisions, exploring new ideas, or simply need a fresh perspective. And like any great board, they bring diverse viewpoints that challenge my assumptions, broaden my thinking, and help me stay grounded while continuing to grow. Some offer strategic advice, while others provide emotional support, creative ideas, or a well-timed reality check when I need it most.

THE POWER OF CONTRASTING PERSPECTIVES

One of the greatest gifts my Personal Board of Advisors offers is balance. As my life and work evolve, new voices join the conversation, bringing fresh ideas and perspectives, while others remain steady, offering timeless wisdom. My friend Dan often encourages me to slow down, ask a lot of questions, and carefully weigh my options before making a move. On the other hand, my daughter Declan inspires me to forge ahead with confidence and not look back. This unique balance keeps me from rushing blindly or hesitating too long, ensuring I'm not just moving fast—but moving with intention. Growth isn't just about charging ahead. It's about knowing when to pause, reflect, and consider the bigger picture.

THE BOARD IN ACTION
CONTRASTING ADVICE THAT LED TO CLARITY

A few years ago, I faced a major career crossroads: take an in-house position after a decade of independent consulting or continue on my own path, which had been less than lackluster during and post-pandemic. As I often do with big decisions, I reached out to my Personal Board of Advisors.

My friend Gabe immediately saw the opportunity: "The timing is perfect," he said. "This role will let you reinvent yourself in the industry in a completely new way." His enthusiasm focused on growth potential and market timing.

Later that same day, over coffee with my friend Scott, I got a completely different take. "How will you differentiate what this company offers in such a crowded market?" he asked, pushing me to consider the practical challenges I'd face.

Both perspectives were precisely what I needed—Gabe's optimism about possibilities balanced with Scott's pragmatic assessment of obstacles. I ultimately took the job, which became a tremendous growth period for me professionally, even though it didn't last long-term. Without those contrasting viewpoints, I might have made the decision with only half the picture, missing critical insights that helped me navigate both the opportunity and its challenges.

This example is precisely why a diverse Personal Board of Advisors matters—different voices illuminate different aspects of important decisions, creating a more complete understanding than any single perspective could provide.

CONTRASTING VIEWPOINTS KEEP YOU FROM MAKING DECISIONS WITH ONLY HALF THE PICTURE.

BUILDING YOUR OWN PERSONAL BOARD OF ADVISORS

If you haven't already, take a moment to think about who's on your Personal Board of Advisors. Who do you turn to when you need support, help solving a problem, or a fresh perspective? Your board doesn't have to be made up of formal mentors or experts—it can include friends who offer honest feedback, colleagues who challenge your thinking, or even people whose stories inspire you from afar.

The beauty of a Personal Board of Advisors is that it's uniquely yours—and it can evolve over time as your needs change. You have the power to "build" it in a way that supports your growth, keeps you grounded, and guides you through life's twists and turns.

BECOMING A MENTOR

Over the years, through my involvement at the University of Texas and Columbia Business School, I've had numerous opportunities to mentor groups of students, hop on one-on-one phone calls, or connect over Zoom. Through friends of our kids and even family connections, I meet with young people all the time. In fact, I rarely say no.

Why? Because I've learned, time and time again, that when we become mentors ourselves, things align—and we learn even more deeply. Effective mentoring isn't about having all the answers. It's about being a thought partner, asking a lot of questions, and helping people unlock opportunities they didn't even know existed.

When I mentor others, I try to wear multiple hats—sometimes, I'm a role model, at other times, a coach, and occasionally a sponsor who opens doors. But the approach that works best is being "a guide by their side." I've found that leading with thoughtful questions helps people discover their own answers.

My goal is to provide a zoomed-out point of view—helping them to see options they might miss when they're caught in the details. I show them different possible paths, point out potential stumbling blocks, and highlight doors they might not have noticed.

While most of my mentoring relationships have developed organically (as research shows is true for over 60% of these relationships), I also encourage exploring formal mentorship programs within organizations for added exposure and structure.

The goal of mentoring is simple: try to make someone's day—or life—a little better than it was before you connected.

HELPING MENTEES FIND THEIR VALUE

Vinay is a friend of my daughter's—a bright, hardworking young man whose first-generation immigrant parents from India had sacrificed everything to give him an opportunity. He put himself through college working two jobs while living in a campus co-op (an affordable community housing option for out-of-state and international students), but was approaching graduation with little guidance and even less confidence in his own worth.

Our first few conversations on Zoom were brief, with Vinay being understandably reserved. But over time, through my questions and point of view, I helped him recognize the tremendous accomplishments he had achieved and the value he had to offer. Through our work together, Vinay completely transformed how he presented himself. We rebuilt his resume from scratch, crafted compelling cover letters that conveyed his unique value, and spent hours on Zoom doing mock interviews where I challenged him with the toughest questions I could think of. I watched him evolve from nervous and uncertain during interviews to confident and articulate—ready to tell his remarkable story with the pride it deserved.

What struck me most was that Vinay didn't see what I saw in him—while earning two degrees from the University of Texas, he managed a campus bar and simultaneously handled meal planning and budgeting for a 200-resident co-op, creating three daily meals on just $8 per person. He was one of the most resourceful people with extraordinary potential I had ever met.

With a clearer view of his own self-worth, Vinay became more selective about his opportunities, declining multiple job offers that wouldn't support his long-term growth. He eventually landed a senior analyst position at a Fortune 500 company, two tiers above his contemporaries, that paid 15% more than his first job offers and enabled him to take his parents all over the world—something that was financially impossible previously.

Today, Vinay and I still connect regularly. Our conversations have evolved beyond career decisions to broader life topics—personal development, fitness goals, reading lists, and financial planning. I've become his accountability partner in many ways, but the truth is, watching his journey unfold has taught me just as much as I've shared with him.

COMMUNITIES AS MENTORS

Sometimes, the best mentors aren't individuals—they're the communities we immerse ourselves in. I've learned that surrounding myself with the right people, focused on a common goal, can be just as powerful as one-on-one mentorship.

Meet my cold plunge group. Every single day in the winter, no matter how freezing it is outside, we plunge into icy water together. This "squad" transforms what feels impossible into something that is actually fun! We cheer each other on and show up—day after day—because we know that when we do it together, we're so much stronger.

There's something magical about collective accountability. When a group of people is waiting for you at the lake, rain or shine, you show up. It's not because any single person would judge your absence, but because that collective expectation becomes a powerful force in your life. You don't want to let the group down, and somehow, that motivation runs deeper than just keeping a promise to yourself.

What sets our cold plunge group apart is that the learning happens through doing, not talking. Nobody stands around giving motivational speeches about embracing discomfort—they just get in the water. I'll never forget watching James get straight into the 38-degree lake his first time without even flinching. Something clicked in my brain at that moment. All my excuses about not being able to handle the cold suddenly felt completely ridiculous.

For me, the real magic of community mentorship comes from our deep human need to belong. I've noticed we don't just push ourselves for personal growth—we do it to stay connected to the people who matter. When my alarm goes off at 6:30 a.m. for Saturday morning swim practice, and I just want to stay in bed, it's not just about improving my stroke; it's because my teammates are waiting and expect me to show up. When I'm shaking through a difficult yoga pose, and my muscles are on fire, it's the energy of everyone around me that keeps me from giving up. We challenge ourselves because we want to remain valued members of these communities that have come to mean so much to us.

THE MAGIC OF MENTORSHIP

What has surprised me most is that in every mentoring relationship, I end up being both teacher and student. When I help others navigate challenges, my own thinking becomes clearer. When I offer perspective, I gain new insights.

This is the true magic of mentorship—it's never just one-way. It's a continuous cycle where wisdom flows freely between people, enriching both lives through the simple act of showing up for each other.

LESSONS LEARNED

- **MENTORSHIP FLOWS BOTH WAYS—**
  Some of my most profound growth has come from conversations where I was supposedly the one doing the teaching. Don't limit yourself to just receiving or just giving—the real magic happens in the exchange.

- **YOUR MENTORS ARE EVERYWHERE IF YOU'RE PAYING ATTENTION—**
  Some of my greatest mentors had no idea they were mentoring me. My kids, colleagues I barely knew, friends over coffee, or even strangers in passing—they've all offered exactly what I needed, exactly when I needed it. The key is staying open and recognizing wisdom wherever it appears.

- **YOU NEED DIFFERENT VOICES IN YOUR CORNER—**
  My Personal Board of Advisors works because it isn't an echo chamber. I need Dan telling me to slow down and think things through just as much as I need Declan pushing me to trust my gut and take the leap. Those contrasting perspectives have saved me time and again from one-sided decisions.

- **COMMUNITIES CAN MENTOR JUST AS POWERFULLY AS INDIVIDUALS—**
  My cold plunge squad, swim team, and yoga community have taught me lessons that no single mentor could. There's something special about the collective energy, shared accountability, and diverse modeling you get from a community that is all working toward similar goals.

- **TEACHING CLARIFIES YOUR OWN THINKING IN SURPRISING WAYS—**
  Whenever I mentor someone else, I find my own thoughts becoming sharper and more organized. Having to articulate advice or guidance forces me to distill what I really believe and what really works.

- **THE UNPLANNED MOMENTS MATTER MOST—**
  The mentorship exchanges that have truly changed lives (mine and others) weren't scheduled or formal. They happened in doorways, on walks between meetings, or over quick cups of coffee. There's a special power in those authentic, unscripted moments of connection.

- **OPENNESS MULTIPLIES IMPACT—**
  The more receptive I've become to both giving and receiving guidance, the more profoundly these relationships have shaped my life and

work. Staying curious and humble creates space for mentorship to work its magic.

- **RECOGNIZE AND HONOR YOUR MENTORS, EVEN SILENTLY—**
  I've found that simply acknowledging to myself who my mentors have been—even those who don't know they've played that role—deepens my appreciation for their influence and helps me actually apply their wisdom rather than just hear it.

QUESTIONS FOR REFLECTION

1. Who makes up your Personal Board of Advisors? List the key people whose guidance and perspectives you value most. What unique strength does each person bring?

   _____
   _____
   _____

2. Who might consider you as their mentor, even if you don't formally hold that title? How might your everyday actions and words be influencing others?

   _____
   _____
   _____

3. What unexpected sources of wisdom have shaped your thinking? Consider moments when insight came from surprising places—children, brief encounters, or seemingly unrelated experiences.

_____

_____

_____

4. Where are the gaps in your Personal Board of Advisors? What perspectives or expertise might be missing that could help balance your decision-making?

_____

_____

_____

5. How do you currently honor and acknowledge those who have mentored you? Are there mentors you should thank or reconnect with?

_____

_____

_____

6. What communities do you belong to that provide collective mentorship? How do these groups challenge and support your growth?

   _____

   _____

   _____

7. What barriers prevent you from seeking mentorship when you need it? Is it pride, fear, or simply not recognizing when guidance would be valuable?

   _____

   _____

   _____

8. In what areas of your life or work could you benefit from intentionally seeking mentorship? What specific challenges might a mentor help you navigate?

   _____

   _____

   _____

9. How might you create more space to mentor others? What knowledge or experience do you have that others might benefit from?

10. What one step could you take this week to either strengthen an existing mentorship relationship or create a new one?

f o u r t e e n

OFF-RAMP TO ENTREPRENEURSHIP

"Rock bottom became the solid foundation on which I rebuilt my life."

J.K. ROWLING

THE SUDDEN DETOUR

In just one conversation, everything I knew for 25 years was gone ...

In Chapter One, I shared how, after twelve years as an officer and at the height of my career, I was on track for what many assumed was next—Chief Merchant, maybe even President. Instead, I was fired by Pete Nordstrom. Despite consistently outperforming our competitive set and the broader industry, the business was under pressure. The board decided one of us had to go. And with his name on the door, it wasn't going to be him.

I came home that day to meet Sam at our house, mid-remodel, and headed straight to yoga. I needed to move. I needed to breathe.

The next day, there was no thank-you, no farewell—just boxes waiting for me on the loading dock, packed by my assistant. Ironically, it was the receiving manager who showed more grace than any executive or Nordstrom family member.

It felt like going from the fast lane—winning every race—to being unceremoniously kicked out of the pool and off the team. I had never been down this road, never swum in this lane, never worn this "suit." It was unfamiliar, uncomfortable—and for a moment, I was completely unmoored.

Just before our third child was born, I had been promoted to EVP of Women's Wear, tripling my fiscal responsibility. I embraced the challenge wholeheartedly—digging deep, engaging external experts, and leading a complete transformation of the women's division. Over time, I grew the business from $1.5 B to $2 B, increased the gross margin by $90 M, and transformed what had been a weakness into a core strength of the company. Even during the 2008 recession, I earned several peer-nominated awards, including the WWD Rising Star award.

Being fired felt like the end of everything I'd worked for, but it turned out to be the beginning of something far better.

It gave me the freedom to rebuild my career and my life with renewed purpose.

But the journey from that moment of shock to finding my new path wasn't straightforward. Standing there, watching decades of dedication distilled into cardboard boxes, I couldn't yet see that this abrupt detour would lead me somewhere I never expected—and somewhere I would ultimately thrive. I was heading down a road I had never been on, and to say it felt awkward is an understatement.

THE UNEXPECTED OPPORTUNITY

I had no plans of starting a business or being an entrepreneur. I actually never really thought logically about leaving Nordstrom, and if I did, perhaps a job at Amazon would have been more likely.

But here I was. I didn't want to work for anyone else. I didn't want to take up tennis, and I needed to work—and I wanted to, if not immediately, then eventually for sure.

So, over the course of a couple of weeks, I called many of the designers and executives at the brands we did business with to tell them I was no longer with Nordstrom. They knew, but I wanted to tell them personally. Simultaneously, my phone began ringing off the hook. My efforts to always collaborate, take time for meetings, and be respectful and transparent were paying off—in spades. Before long, I had half a dozen brands asking if I could work for them as a consultant to help protect and navigate their Nordstrom business in my absence. One denim brand, whose business we had grown exponentially, wanted my help planning for and forecasting the infamous Nordstrom Anniversary sale, as they had nearly 25% of their annual revenue at stake during this two-week time frame. Additionally, a senior partner from Boston Consulting Group, who helped me solve multiple business challenges, offered me a position to join their team as a Senior Advisor and North American Retail Expert.

All of this sounded great, but I needed a little infrastructure to say "yes" and get started. I called a friend who did branding and packaging for national and international brands, and she agreed to meet with me. We worked through ideas to create my brand, Loretta Soffe Consulting. We picked colors and fonts, created a brand symbol, and designed my website. True to Nordstrom training, I insisted on branded stationery so I could send out handwritten thank-you notes— which I still do.

While she was helping me get the logistics in place, I was reaching out and learning what to charge and how to structure contracts. I had no idea. Early on, I learned a few hard lessons when I didn't specify important details in the "Exhibit A" portion of a contract, and those mistakes nearly cost me $50K. I asked for contract samples, pitch decks, and PowerPoints from friends who had done this longer than I had. I figured, *why do this from scratch if I can copy and edit from someone who had already done it before me?*

In the weeks and months that followed, I learned how to craft a scope of work, timelines, deliverables, and most importantly, clear contracts. I let people know I was ready and able to work.

I was in Cabo with my family when a good friend from the industry called me about a joint venture between a European brand and American Express. She was the CMO, leading their launch strategy in the US, and with their team almost entirely from Paris, she needed someone who understood the US market, knew the brands, and had relationships to help secure distribution. I was the unicorn they were looking for. I didn't know what to charge as a consulting fee, but I knew what my intellectual property was worth, and I understood what they needed. I made a detailed proposal outlining my unique value and the deliverables they could expect, and they didn't blink. It was my first and best contract, negotiated right from the beach.

For vendors in New York and Los Angeles, I was addressing the problems I had solved most of my career—expanding categories, identifying new channels, whether in stores or e-commerce, and improving inventory management and merchandise assortments. I provided leadership development, mentoring shoulder to shoulder, and helped guide total transformations and organizational restructures.

As a Senior Advisor for BCG, I had the privilege of bringing my experience and insights (having had the "job") to their retail clients around the world. The Nordstrom reputation was so strong that I was invited into boardrooms in India, Indonesia, Hong Kong, Melbourne, Finland, and Canada to help companies improve their business. That was one of the most unexpected benefits.

For McKinsey, I led a merchandise fundamentals course for an entire day to 250 non-English speaking buyers, financial planners, and merchandisers using a translator in China. Imagine saying wedding vows where the priest says it, and you repeat it with a pause in between each statement. Trust me when I say there must have been a lot lost in translation that day because there were times when the whole audience erupted in laughter, and I still have no idea why.

NO LONGER "LORETTA FROM NORDSTROM"

But it wasn't all rosy. There were plenty of times when I would get a call—totally unexpected—to inform me that budgets were being cut and so was my consulting contract.

The worst was when I was newly self-employed and in New York during February Fashion Week. I was used to having a car, a driver, and all the best seats at shows and dinner dates at all the best restaurants. This trip was different. I was no longer "Loretta from Nordstrom"—I was just Loretta. Traveling solo, trying to catch an Uber or a taxi in a torrential downpour. There were no cars to be had, so I walked most of my way back to the hotel, arriving with waterlogged boots and hair that looked like I just got out of the pool.

OFF-RAMP TO ENTREPRENEURSHIP

My phone was dead. I powered it up only to learn that my dinner date, a good industry friend, had canceled our Valentine's dinner. Disappointed and hungry, I opted for some nuts from the bodega next door to my hotel and decided to go to yoga. I went across town, fortunately in an Uber (with surge pricing), to the studio, only to discover I had arrived at the wrong studio. I decided to stay and proceeded to be yelled at by the super-rigid Bikram instructor. With tears in my eyes, I finished the class and lay down in Savasana, reflecting on my new reality. It's at times like this that if you don't focus on the good things, you will go down the drain.

As I lay there in that unfamiliar studio, dripping with sweat and alone, I thought about that day I went to yoga right after being fired—how I'd needed to breathe. Now, here I was, breathing again, but this time on my own terms. The irony wasn't lost on me: sometimes, you have to lose everything you thought defined you to discover who you really are.

Standing in that loading dock with my career packed in boxes had felt like the end. But now, even on this miserable Valentine's Day in New York, I understood that being kicked out of the pool didn't mean I'd forgotten how

SOMETIMES, YOU HAVE TO LOSE EVERYTHING YOU THOUGHT DEFINED YOU TO DISCOVER WHO YOU REALLY ARE.

to swim. It just meant I'd found a different body of water—one where I could chart my own course.

THE ART OF BALANCING MULTIPLE ROLES

That pivotal moment—going from the top to suddenly being out—reshaped how I define success, failure, and resilience.

What I came to realize was that I had been holding down three full-time jobs all along: executive, mother, and wife. In hindsight, it's clear: balance is bullshit. I wasn't striving for some perfect split between work, motherhood, and marriage; I was making conscious choices, sometimes hard ones, and trusting that what mattered most would rise to the top. It wasn't always graceful, but it was always mine. The hard truth? There's no way to be a perfect 10/10 in all three at once. Real success comes from knowing when to lead in each role—and having the courage to ask for help, delegate, and build a strong support system around you.

> I WAS MAKING CONSCIOUS CHOICES, SOMETIMES HARD ONES, AND TRUSTING THAT WHAT MATTERED MOST WOULD RISE TO THE TOP.

"Doing it all" has to mean more than just crushing it at work.

Because I never over-identified with my job or title, the transition—while painful—didn't break me. What emerged from that corporate ending was a rediscovery of what mattered most. The consulting work that came my way brought unexpected joy and freedom. And the parts of life I had sidelined—family, health, presence—took center stage in the most fulfilling way. For the first time since our eldest child was born, I was able to prioritize being a mom.

I've found that balancing life, career, motherhood, and health comes down to three key elements: clarity, courage, and commitment.

- CLARITY is about knowing your values and priorities—what truly matters most to you. Without it, it's easy to get swept up in the demands and pressures of the moment.

- COURAGE is the strength to speak up and protect those values, set boundaries, and advocate for yourself.

- COMMITMENT is about staying true to yourself, your partner, and your family—showing up fully in all areas of your life.

The greatest lesson? Worry less about strategizing your career path and more about doing your best in the job you're in. When I embraced this philosophy, I found myself navigating Sam's established family routines, finding my place in the children's daily schedules, and discovering joy in the simple moments of after-school snacks and carpools—all while Sam embarked on his own new career in real estate.

This reinvention ultimately led to the most fulfilling chapter of my professional life, one that finally aligned with my core values of family, flexibility, and genuine happiness.

THE BLESSING IN DISGUISE

Looking back now, what felt like the worst day of my professional life—standing on that loading dock, watching my career get packed into boxes—became the catalyst for my greatest transformation. That forced detour pushed me off a path I might never have left on my own, and onto one that led to deeper fulfillment than I could have imagined.

The strength and resilience I discovered in myself surprised me. The freedom and flexibility I had always craved became a reality, allowing me to take summers off with my children and be present for the moments that matter most. I gained crystal clarity about my values, priorities, and goals. From the disruption emerged an intentional life—one where success is measured not by title or salary, but by alignment with what truly matters.

LESSONS LEARNED

- **YOUR CAREER DOESN'T DEFINE YOU—**
  I didn't over-identify with my job or title, which made the transition possible.

- **BUILD RELATIONSHIPS THAT OUTLAST YOUR TITLE—**
  The calls that came after I left Nordstrom didn't come because of my role—they came because of the relationships I'd built and the trust I'd earned. Titles come and go, but the people who know your character? That's your real résumé.

- **BE WILLING TO START FROM SCRATCH—**
  From pricing my services to negotiating contracts, I had to learn things no executive role had ever prepared me for. A new chapter requires new skills.

- **KNOW YOUR WORTH: WITHOUT THE LOGO BEHIND YOU—**
  When you truly understand your value, you can ask for what you deserve—with clarity and confidence—even from a beach chair in Cabo.

- **GET COMFORTABLE BEING UNCOMFORTABLE—**
  Those quiet, lonely moments in New York reminded me that growth rarely feels good at first. But if you stick with it, what starts as discomfort becomes something powerful.

- **BALANCE IS BULLSHIT—**
  You can't give 100% to everything at once. The real skill is knowing where to lean in, when to let go, and how to stay grounded in what matters most.

- **TRUST THAT SOMETHING BETTER IS COMING—**
  What feels like the end might just be a course correction. Sometimes, the universe clears the path before you even know you're meant to take a new one. Stay the course— it's leading somewhere worth going.

QUESTIONS FOR REFLECTION

1. Have you ever felt too defined by your job title? What would your identity look like without it?

   _____

   _____

   _____

2. What relationships have you built that would survive a major career transition?

   _____

   _____

   _____

3. If you were suddenly fired tomorrow, what would be your first three phone calls and why?

   _____

   _____

   _____

4. What's one area of your life where you're trying to be a perfect 10/10, and where might you benefit from adjusting your expectations?

   _____

   _____

   _____

5. Think about a time when a setback led to an unexpected opportunity. What did you learn about yourself?

   _____

   _____

   _____

6. What values do you want to prioritize in your next chapter? Are there boundaries you need to set to protect them?

_____

_____

_____

7. If you could negotiate your ideal work-life arrangement, what would it look like?

_____

_____

_____

fifteen

OUR SECRET

*"Find someone you can hold onto.
Find someone who'll be there for you.
'Cause that's all that really matters in the end."*

TEDDY SWIMS

OUR FORMULA AFTER 25 YEARS OF MARRIAGE
COINS, COMPROMISE, AND COMMITMENT

When seventy-six dollars in spare change is all that stands between you and an empty refrigerator during your first week of marriage, you learn quickly that financial partnership isn't just about money—it's about resourcefulness, trust, and unwavering teamwork.

THE FOUNDATION OF PARTNERSHIP

Sam and I were married in Mexico, creating our dream wedding on a $12,000 budget we mostly paid for ourselves. When we got home from our honeymoon, reality hit: our bank accounts were completely empty. But instead of panicking, we grabbed the giant change jar we'd been filling for months. Together, we lugged it to the grocery store and fed pennies and nickels into the machine—walking away with $76 and just enough groceries to get us through the week.

We could've stressed or pointed fingers. Instead, we laughed. That moment became a metaphor for how we would do life together: make do with what we have, stay optimistic, and find a way forward—together.

From the beginning, we took our commitment seriously. This wasn't just a wedding—it was the start of a real partnership. Before we even said "I do," we had merged our finances, aligned on our dreams, and chosen to back each other completely. We haven't had to dip into a coin jar since, but the philosophy stuck: when things get hard, don't panic. Stay grounded. Stay united. Find the solution, not the problem.

That week taught us something lasting.

Real marriage isn't about equal effort every day—it's about aligned effort over time. Some days, one of us carried more; other days, the roles reversed. But we never kept score.

We trusted that the other person was doing their best, and we stayed focused on the bigger picture we were building together.

We didn't chase balance. We built trust. We didn't split everything 50/50—we each gave 100% to the whole. Not always at the same time, not in the same way, but always with the same intention: *us.*

Balance is bullshit. It sets you up to feel like you're failing on both sides.

Partnership is everything. It gives you the freedom to shift, to grow, to show up for each other fully—especially when life doesn't go according to plan.

Through every high and low, we've adjusted, supported, and honored each other's individuality while continuing to move forward as a team. That's been our foundation for 25 years—and it's what's kept us thriving.

ROOTED AND SURROUNDED
WHO YOU CHOOSE MATTERS

We haven't navigated this journey alone. From the beginning, we've surrounded ourselves with people who reflected the kind of life and love we aspired to build. Sam's parents, in particular, modeled a marriage grounded in respect, humor, and shared responsibility. Their example gave us a living blueprint—one we observed closely and learned from.

Beyond family, we've intentionally sought out couples who were further down the road—real-life mentors who shared their wisdom without sugarcoating the hard parts. Their stories and support helped shape our perspective and gave us hope during the tougher seasons.

And throughout our 25 years together, we've continued to invest in relationships that bring out the best in us—friends who fill our cups, challenge us, and celebrate life's wins alongside us.

Most of all, we've prioritized *us*. We've always spent a lot of time together—not just under the same roof, but truly present with one another. That deliberate choice—to nurture our relationship, to learn from those who've walked ahead, and to face every challenge as a united front—has been a major part of what's kept our marriage thriving.

FINANCIAL PARTNERSHIP

After we got engaged, we opened our first joint bank account. I brought credit card debt and a credit score that was a little embarrassing, while Sam, pure to his form, came with real estate investments shared with college friends and virtually no credit card debt. Despite these differences, we never questioned whether to combine our finances. Our partnership started at the bank, even before it was formalized at the altar. From day one, our money belonged to both of us—no matter who had it or earned it.

OUR SECRET

We bought our first home—our current home—before we were married, borrowing $30K from Sam's parents for the down payment and paying them back within a couple of years. It was a small, historic house full of charm but in need of updates. When our family started to grow, we made one of our best decisions: we moved into Sam's parents' basement during the renovation.

Declan slept in a converted workshop, and Hank's bassinet fit snugly beside our bed. It was tight, but the experience bonded all of us in unexpected ways. Mornings became a special ritual—Declan would take her bottle and head upstairs to climb into bed with Grandma Colleen. They'd read stories, play with jewelry, and chat about her travels. It's no wonder Declan became a globetrotter.

During my Nordstrom years, there were times when we felt "wealthy" after some big bonus checks. We could have given in to the temptation to buy a bigger, fancier house—we could afford the mortgage. But we didn't. We stayed in the home we'd built together because it was enough. It held our memories, our milestones, and our values. We chose heart and soul over square footage.

We've always made financial decisions together—deciding how much to save, when to spend, and how to celebrate the wins. Sometimes, that meant a weekend away, a nice dinner, or even a piece of jewelry. But regardless of who brought in the paycheck or how big the bonus was, we never saw money as "his" or "mine." It was always *ours*—from day one.

Our approach wasn't about control or comparison; it was about trust, transparency, and shared priorities.

That mindset served us especially well during the lean years—like COVID, when both of our businesses came to a halt, and our income dropped to zero almost overnight. We didn't panic because we had never overextended ourselves in the good times. Living below our means was a habit shaped by how we were both raised, and it allowed us to ride out tough seasons without resentment or fear.

Through it all—booms and busts—our financial philosophy stayed the same: stay grounded, stay united, and make decisions in service of the life we're building together. Money, for us, has always been a tool—not a scoreboard.

> MONEY, FOR US, HAS ALWAYS BEEN A TOOL—NOT A SCOREBOARD.

We naturally fell into complementary financial roles that played to our strengths. When Sam was home with the kids, and I was working and traveling, he took the lead on paying the bills and managing the day-to-day logistics. I focused more on creating memories—planning travel, experiences, and the kinds of moments that anchor a family.

Over time, we found a rhythm that worked. Sam keeps a close eye on our financial stability and long-term planning, while I bring the perspective of how we want to *live*—not just what we want to save. We respect each other's lens and usually land somewhere in the middle. He's grown to appreciate the value of the experiences I prioritize, and I've come to truly value his more conservative, steady approach.

It's never been about who's "better with money." It's about bringing our strengths to the table—and building a life that reflects both of us.

DIVISION OF LABOR
TRUE PARTNERSHIP

Getting married after 30 helped. We had both lived alone and were used to doing everything ourselves. So when we got married, and life got busy, we naturally split things up and just made it work.

When we started having kids and made the decision that Sam would step away from his career to stay home, it was one of the boldest, most defining shifts we made as a couple. At the time, it wasn't common—and we didn't know anyone else doing it. But it felt right for us. We weren't following a script. We were creating our own blueprint.

Sam took the lead on everything at home—grocery runs, dry cleaning, laundry, and keeping the house in order. He handled all the details I simply didn't have the time or margin to think about, especially during the years when I was fully immersed in leading a $2B business and constantly on the road. Truthfully, I didn't do much on the domestic front during that season.

But we protected our weekends fiercely—ski days, swims in the lake, and just being together. That was our reset button. Our time to reconnect and remember what we were doing all this for.

What made it all work was Sam's willingness to fully own that role—not as a backup plan, but as a deliberate choice. He gave me the freedom to go all in at work without constantly looking over my shoulder or wondering if things were falling apart at home. Because they weren't. He had it covered. And that allowed me to be fully present with the kids—and with him—when I was home.

We were both giving 100%—just in different lanes.

It's easy in any marriage to fall into the trap of thinking *you're* doing more than the other person. That quiet scorekeeping can creep in, and if you're not careful, it becomes a real source of resentment. I was never in a book club, but I used to joke that most book clubs weren't really about the book—they were about venting. From what I heard, the conversation often turned into a laundry list of what husbands *weren't* doing at home.

We were lucky to avoid a lot of that tension—not because our setup was perfect, but because of how we approached it. We each had seasons of carrying more, and we trusted that the other person was doing their best. That became our unspoken mantra: *"They're doing the best they can."* And honestly, that mindset saved us more times than I can count. It allowed us to move through the hard parts with more grace—and a lot less keeping score.

As the kids got older and my career shifted, I had more time and flexibility, so I naturally took on more of the day-to-day at home. But Sam still runs point on errands—he's always willing to restock the fridge, pick up the dry cleaning, and get things checked off the list. We don't overthink it. We just acknowledge what needs to be done and divide and conquer.

Somewhere along the way, Sam became surprisingly great at hosting. I like to joke that I trained him well, but the truth is, he picked up the art of it all on his own. He's got the charcuterie board down, knows how to set the vibe with music and lighting, and always has the bar ready before guests arrive. He's more than just helpful—he's genuinely good at it. Over time, he became proficient at a lot of things around the house—way beyond the basics.

He also knows the little things that make me feel calm and cared for—like a clean house, a made bed, and folded laundry. I'm perfectly capable of doing those things, but he does them because he knows they matter to me. And in return, I'm oddly enthusiastic about using the leaf blower to clear the driveway. Go figure.

We've never labeled tasks as "his" or "hers." To us, it's just life stuff. If it needs doing, we do it. That attitude has shaped our kids, too. They've grown up seeing partnership, not roles—and it's made our home run more smoothly and more joyfully.

That flexibility in how we divide things has been one of the quiet secrets to our longevity. We've adapted with each season, stepping up when the other needed support. We never kept score. We just kept showing up for each other. That lack of rigidity has given us more time, more peace, and more room to grow—together.

FAMILY FIRST
UNITED IN OUR COMMITMENT

They say when you marry someone, you marry their family—and in our case, that couldn't be more true.

Sam has one sister and two nieces, and I've always been their go-to for everything from life advice to outfit choices. On my side, I'm the youngest of five, with ten nieces and nephews—and Sam didn't just show up for birthdays or holidays. He showed up for the real stuff. He could have easily stayed on the sidelines at basketball games or during chaotic family gatherings, but instead, he pulled up a front-row seat. Whether it was career advice, helping someone move cross-country, or navigating a tough decision, Sam was there—with his calm, thoughtful presence and that quiet way he has of making everything feel a little more manageable.

It might seem like a side note to our relationship, but it's actually the opposite. His steady, all-in love for my family only deepened my love for him. That kind of selflessness leaves an impression.

OUR SECRET

Over time, he became *their* person, too. For most of my siblings and their kids, Sam is the one they call when they need help, clarity, or just someone who will follow through. When my dad was in the final days of his life with Alzheimer's, Sam didn't just support me—he supported all of us. He sat with us at the hospice center for nearly 48 hours straight, managing food and drinks so we didn't have to leave my dad's side.

When one of my nephews got married, he and his bride asked Sam to officiate. When another nephew passed away far too young, Sam was the one they asked to emcee his memorial. He's not just my husband. He's their rock, their guide, their constant.

He didn't marry *into* my family—he *became* part of it. And that, more than anything, has shown me what real partnership looks like.

Where extended family can often divide a marriage, for us, it's been a source of strength. We haven't pulled away—we've leaned in, together. Through the joyful moments and the heartbreaking ones, we've faced family as a united front. That approach has deepened our connection in ways I never could have predicted. It's taught us to communicate better, love harder, and model real commitment for our kids.

Sam didn't just marry me—he chose to invest fully in the people I came from. And that choice, time and again, has reminded me I chose exactly the right partner.

There's no such thing as perfect balance when it comes to two families. You can't divide your time or your heart evenly—and we never tried to. A lot of couples avoid hard conversations to keep the peace. We had them to build it. That's the thing about long-term partnership—it's never about perfect balance. **Balance is bullshit.** It's about showing up for each other, especially when things get complicated.

COMMUNICATION AND VULNERABILITY
GROWING TOGETHER

In the early days of our relationship, it was all about building that team mentality—aligning around the big stuff, supporting each other, and having each other's back. But as the years went on, what became even more important was how we communicated. Not just the logistics of who's picking up the kids or paying the bills, but the real stuff—feelings, frustrations, expectations.

Sam and I have very different styles when it comes to communication. I have what I call an "Irish reaction"—when something bothers me, I tend to speak up right away. I feel it; I say it. My expectations are high—of myself and the people I love—and if they're not met, I can get sharp without meaning to. Sam, on the other hand, rarely complains. He keeps things in until he doesn't. He'll absorb a lot before letting me know something's been bothering him.

We've had to work through this dynamic over the years. And the truth is, we're still working on it. One moment that sticks with me happened on a walk—we were facing traffic, and he reached out and grabbed my arm to keep me safe. I snapped, "Don't grab me like that!" His intentions were good—he was trying to protect me—but my reaction came out wrong. I could see him go quiet, and it wasn't until hours later that he finally told me how much it hurt his feelings.

That one moment taught me a lot. I could be more aware of my tone. He could speak up sooner. And together, we could keep building a rhythm that works better for both of us.

After 26 years, you'd think we'd have it all figured out—but the truth is, communication is something we're constantly learning. The difference is now we know how to come back to each other with more grace, more curiosity, and a lot more compassion. We're not perfect—we're just committed to getting better.

INTIMACY AND CONNECTION
BEYOND TEAMWORK

You can be a team—share responsibilities, make decisions together, co-parent, even communicate openly—but without physical connection, what you have is a great friendship, not a great marriage. For us, intimacy has always been a cornerstone of our relationship.

In the early years, it was all unfiltered lust and late-night spontaneity. But over time—between babies, demanding jobs, and endless to-do lists—we had to be more intentional about making space for that connection. We still prioritized it, but it took effort. And Sam? Let's just say he was never shy about pointing out when it had been too long.

Later in life, with more time and fewer distractions, we've rediscovered each other in ways that feel deeper and more grounded. It's not about checking a box—it's about staying close, curious, and connected.

One way we keep the spark alive is by carving out time with no plans. Just the two of us, making dinner, talking, watching a movie, or simply sitting together. For me, that's the foundation for intimacy—feeling emotionally connected before anything else. Sam's learned that when the house is clean, the laundry is done, and my brain can quiet down, the rest of me can turn on. And I've learned that for him, closeness often starts with physical touch—but it's even better when it's built on real connection.

We've learned that intimacy isn't something you schedule and check off a list. You don't balance your way into connection—you build it, moment by moment.

YOU DON'T BALANCE YOUR WAY INTO CONNECTION— YOU BUILD IT, MOMENT BY MOMENT.

OUR SECRET

THE TEAM APPROACH TO MARRIAGE

Looking back over 25 years, it's clear that our foundation of mutual respect and shared effort has allowed us to thrive through every season. Whether it was navigating my demanding executive career while Sam managed our home and kids, weathering financial ups and downs, or walking through family crises—we always faced life side by side.

What makes our partnership strong isn't that we avoided challenges—we've faced plenty. It's that we chose to face them *together.* We respected each other's strengths, stepped in where the other needed help, and stayed aligned even when the path ahead felt uncertain. We've been flexible with our roles, honest in our communication, united in our family relationships, and intentional about keeping our connection strong.

The traditional gender roles that shaped generations before us never applied to us. We built our marriage around what actually worked—Sam stepping fully into the role of primary caregiver while I leaned into my career, both of us making financial decisions together and adapting as life shifted. That kind of flexibility became one of our greatest strengths—and it gave our kids a front-row seat to what real partnership looks like.

And here's what we've learned: marriage doesn't work because you find the perfect balance. It works because you stay aligned on what matters most.

Balance is bullshit. Life isn't split 50/50. In some seasons, one of you gives more. In other seasons, the roles reverse. The key is knowing you're in it together—for the long haul.

If there's one lesson we hope others take from our story, it's this: build a partnership where roles are fluid, communication is honest, and the team always comes first. When you both truly want what's best for the *us*—not just the *me*—you create a foundation strong enough to handle whatever life throws your way. From emptying a coin jar for groceries to raising three kids, building careers, and growing together for a quarter century—it's the team that makes it work.

LESSONS LEARNED

- **SHARE FINANCIAL RESPONSIBILITY EQUALLY—** It doesn't matter who earns it; the money belongs to both of you. Make decisions together and live below your means so you can weather the unexpected.

- **EMBRACE ROLE FLEXIBILITY—** Let go of traditional gender roles. Adjust your division of labor based on your life stage, your strengths, and what actually works for your family.

- **GIVE THE BENEFIT OF THE DOUBT—**
  Don't keep score. Assume your partner is doing their best, even when things feel uneven. Trust goes further than tallying tasks.

- **TALK HONESTLY ABOUT FAMILY DYNAMICS—**
  Don't stay silent to avoid conflict. Speak up with kindness, listen without defensiveness, and support each other through the messiness of extended family.

- **ADAPT YOUR COMMUNICATION STYLES—**
  Understand how your partner processes emotion and stress. Practice honest, vulnerable conversations—even (and especially) when it's uncomfortable.

- **PROTECT YOUR INTIMATE CONNECTION—**
  Physical closeness matters. Stay curious about what your partner needs, and speak up about what makes you feel seen, desired, and emotionally safe.

- **FACE CHALLENGES AS A TEAM—**
  Life will throw curveballs. Don't blame—align. A strong partnership makes even the hardest seasons feel manageable.

QUESTIONS FOR REFLECTION

1. How do you and your partner approach financial decisions? Are there any unspoken assumptions about who earns, spends, or manages the money?

   _____

   _____

   _____

2. How do you divide household and parenting responsibilities? Is it working—or is there quiet resentment building?

   _____

   _____

   _____

3. How do you navigate extended family dynamics together? Can you be honest with each other without hurting feelings or avoiding the conversation?

   _____

   _____

   _____

4. What are your different communication styles in conflict? How could you adjust to better hear, support, or understand each other?

_____

_____

_____

5. When life gets busy, how do you stay connected—emotionally and physically?

_____

_____

_____

6. When challenges arise, do you turn toward each other or away? What would help strengthen your *"we before me"* approach?

_____

_____

_____

BUILD A PARTNERSHIP WHERE ROLES ARE FLUID, COMMUNICATION IS HONEST, AND THE TEAM ALWAYS COMES FIRST.

s i x t e e n

RAISING FUTURE LEADERS

"The greatest leaders don't create followers; they create more leaders."

TOM PETERS

FOUNDATIONS
RAISING HUMANS, NOT JUST LEADERS

It was never our intention to "train" our kids in sports or business. Our goal was to raise happy, healthy, respectful humans who made good decisions and treated each other and others well. When they were little, our home was full of love and nurturing, but also discipline and clear boundaries.

As they got older, in high school, we didn't have strict curfews or tons of rules. Instead, we had clear expectations and consequences if they let us down. They didn't wake us up when they got home—I needed my sleep—but occasionally, they did get busted when I would see the light on in the hall in the early hours of the morning. We did not "track" them ... we knew they knew if they were somewhere doing something they shouldn't have, eventually and quickly we would find out. This was an approach Sam's parents took with Sam and his sister KC, and it seemed to work pretty well for them, so we figured we would model that same thing.

The structured environment we created wasn't about control but about preparing them for independence. As they entered their teen years, we shifted our approach. We allowed them to make decisions without constant supervision, trusting them to rise to the occasion, and they almost always did.

THE EARLY LESSONS OF LEADERSHIP

I still remember the afternoon I picked up Declan from middle school, allowing her to skip science class because I needed her help. I was consulting for a major swimwear manufacturer that had just acquired a teen swim and surf brand out of Southern California. As a consultant, I was charged with leading a transformation that included overhauling the brand positioning, identifying and specifying the target customer, understanding the market position, and leading the product assortment strategy.

Who better to help me than Declan, who represented the exact customer we were aspiring to target? So, I picked her up from Islander Middle School, and we went to the local Starbucks, where I proceeded to take the strategy call from my car, phone on speaker, with her in the passenger seat. With the phone on mute, she would listen to the discussion and answer questions about customer behavior, preferences, and priorities by writing answers in her science notebook for me to see from my seat on the driver's side of the car. She helped me answer specifics about styles, color, print, and price by passing notes back and forth to me. This "sanctioned eavesdrop" became her first exposure to brand building and product positioning.

At age 15, Declan founded a social media consulting business, DeccaDotCom, for marketers, business leaders, and entrepreneurs, where she administered seminars, led private workshops, and worked with B2B and B2C clients. She began helping a local boutique owner with Instagram posts and quickly expanded her expertise into a full-fledged consulting business when she recognized that many established business professionals understood their products but struggled with reaching younger audiences on social platforms.

What impressed me most was watching her navigate the balance between her natural creative instincts and the business fundamentals I had exposed her to over the years. By the time she graduated from college, she had built a steady client base that provided both substantial income and invaluable real-world business experience that most people don't acquire until well after college.

That afternoon at Starbucks wasn't just about helping me with a client call—it was an unintended teaching moment. By bringing her into my professional world, I was able to show her that her voice mattered, even as a middle schooler. The seeds planted that day continue to grow as she navigates her own path, armed with real-world skills that most don't encounter until well into adulthood. Leadership development doesn't always happen in formal settings—sometimes, the most powerful lessons come from being in the passenger seat.

EMPATHY AS A FOUNDATION
WHAT GREAT LEADERS ARE MADE OF

Declan's journey from that day at Starbucks to running her own successful business shows how real exposure to business builds real skills. But true leadership isn't limited to business sense; it's also about courage and empathy. I saw these qualities emerge naturally in our son Hank.

Throughout my career, I have learned that some of the most effective leaders are empathetic, curious, and able to unite people. They are also strong in their convictions and have a quiet confidence in leading people and teams. They exude an atmosphere of trust, and people feel safe following their guidance.

RAISING FUTURE LEADERS

Our son Hank attended a football camp in the eighth grade intended to help the kids improve their conditioning and develop a strong team chemistry. Little did he know, it would be one of the first times he would exercise his leadership skills.

When picking teams for a scrimmage at the end of the day, one of the seventh graders was picking on a fourth grader. Luke, the fourth grader, was being told he could not play in the scrimmage because he "sucked." Upon hearing this, Hank instantly stepped in to stop the older guy, and he gladly invited Luke to join his team because Luke really was good, and it was unfair to keep him out. Luke ultimately became a standout high school athlete.

At the time, Hank had no idea what he was doing other than adding a talented player to his team for the day. He knew instinctively that stepping in and stopping the bully was the right thing to do, and he has built on that skill since. Hank never had big leadership titles or roles, but has developed an innate sense of leadership and responsibility to do the right thing for those around him.

Watching Hank stand up for someone vulnerable reminded me of what truly matters in leadership—not just achieving results, but how you achieve them and who you bring along with you. His willingness to risk social capital to protect someone else demonstrated a maturity that many executives spend years trying to develop. As parents, we can't force these moments of character development, but we can recognize and reinforce them when they happen naturally.

THE COMPLETE LEADER
BALANCING PRACTICALITY AND EMPATHY

Leadership comes in different forms, and sometimes, the most essential team member is the one who maintains the perfect balance between getting things done and supporting others emotionally. This is where our youngest child, Ashleigh, shines.

Every team needs someone who just gets shit done. In our family, that person is Ashleigh. She has had the nickname "logistics" for as long as I can remember, and more importantly, since she has been able to fix every TV in our house, program remotes, reset passwords, and build IKEA furniture—that alone gets her MVP status! But logistics isn't her only skill. Ashleigh has become the go-to on our Chapin family team because of her intuition, her ability to know right from wrong, her empathy, and her conviction. She is the one to seek out for advice on tough conversations, important decisions, and overall stuff.

EVERY TEAM NEEDS SOMEONE WHO JUST GETS SHIT DONE.

When Ashleigh was unanimously voted to be captain of her State Championship Lacrosse team, she was put to the test to not only maintain her athletic excellence on the field but also tap into her ability to motivate, inspire, and encourage her teammates to excel on the field and bond off it. The true test came in the end-of-season championship game, when her team, the reigning champions, were blindsided by their opponents and lost against all odds. This was the last game she would play as a senior, and she was naturally incredibly disappointed. But a true leader doesn't get to wallow in their own misery. Ashleigh had to quickly collect herself and offer support to the 20 other girls who were equally disappointed—some crying, some angry, and placing blame on the referees or other players. I'll never forget watching Ashleigh in that moment, on the field, while the other team was celebrating and their fans stormed the field. Ashleigh put her tremendous disappointment aside and instead hugged and counseled her team members.

What struck me most about Ashleigh in that championship moment wasn't just her composure, but I watched proudly as I witnessed her natural understanding that leadership sometimes means putting yourself last. In the corporate world, we often celebrate the visionaries and the strategists, but it's those who can balance technical competence with emotional intelligence who truly make organizations function. Ashleigh embodies this dual capacity—fixing what's broken while also healing what hurts—a leadership quality that can't be taught in business school but is invaluable in any team setting. Her ability to lead through service rather than authority is perhaps the most sophisticated leadership skill of all.

FROM STRUCTURE TO AUTONOMY
MY NORDSTROM LEADERSHIP PHILOSOPHY AT HOME

Throughout my 25-year career at Nordstrom, whether I was managing up or down, I learned that structure creates freedom, and autonomy and control breed success. Research shows that when people have a greater sense of autonomy and control, their stress is reduced, apathy decreases, and they ultimately perform better.

My leadership style, both professionally and as a parent, is to give people enough rope to hang themselves while never hanging them out to dry! I set clear expectations and am always available for support when needed. Whether I was a buyer or an executive, my goal when mentoring the individuals I supported was to teach them to think like I think and see like I see. If they could learn by my example and through questions and answers, they would inevitably not only perform, but excel in my absence.

STRUCTURE CREATES FREEDOM, AUTONOMY AND CONTROL BREED SUCCESS.

BEGINNING WITH THE END IN MIND

One of the most valuable principles I brought from my business experience was thinking broadly and beginning with the end in mind. If you want to grow your $5M business to $25M, put a stake in the ground and work backward. When you do that, you can imagine what success looks like, what you need to do to ensure success, and what the mile markers are along the way. It is *never* a straight line, but this process of starting with a goal and working backward has proven successful dozens and dozens of times.

Whether it's building a brand or creating a life you want, use the "start with the end in mind" approach. It works consistently. I've used this approach with each of our kids through various decisions and stages, whether it was the college application process, creating a personal brand, or running a half-marathon. This process of reverse engineering helped each of them zoom out from the day-to-day, see the bigger picture with a clear focus on their goals, making the incremental steps more logical.

For Hank, we began with his dream of attending the University of Texas. Rather than simply hoping he'd get in, we mapped out what would make his application stand out. Beyond maintaining strong grades, he needed to demonstrate leadership and community involvement and have some unique experiences in order to tell some compelling stories on his application. Together, we identified opportunities that aligned with his interests—mentoring special needs athletes, creating a concession business with his sister during the little league baseball season, and taking on a leadership role for the youth organization at our church. Each experience built upon the last, creating a compelling story that ultimately led to his acceptance letter. The pride he felt wasn't just about the result, but about the path he had navigated with purpose.

For Ashleigh, her half-marathon journey exemplifies this principle perfectly. What started as a casual "I could never do that" comment evolved into a methodical training plan. I encouraged her to map out the 12 weeks leading up to race day, breaking the seemingly impossible 13.1 miles into manageable training increments. Each week built on the previous one, with small victories and inevitable setbacks along the way. When she crossed that finish line, she understood viscerally that most significant achievements aren't about the day of performance, but about the disciplined preparation that makes it possible.

As Declan continues to chart her own unique career path and build her personal brand, we have frequent conversations about what success looks like in 3 to 5 years. Where does she see herself living, how does she see her work evolving, what kinds of brands does she admire and want to align herself with, and what does she want to be known for? It is imagining the future without constraints but with an eye toward the bigger picture that helps create a filter for decision-making today. In order to build something valuable and sustainable, the decisions she makes today need to be well thought out and selective in order to underpin the broader and future vision. And I am proud to say, she is doing just that.

EMBRACING FAILURE
THE HIDDEN LEADERSHIP LESSON

While I've emphasized goal setting and planning throughout this chapter, I would be remiss if I didn't talk about one of the most important pillars of leadership development: failure. We live in such an achievement-oriented culture that we often shy away from talking about our setbacks, yet they've been some of the most powerful experiences for both me and my children.

We've always told our children that failure isn't just okay—it's inevitable and an important part of life. The way we respond to setbacks reveals our character and shapes who we are much more than our highlights and successes.

All of our kids have experienced setbacks and failures. Most recently, for example, Hank applied to a fifth-year master's program at UT. He submitted an excellent application, complete with thoughtful essays, glowing letters from his employer and a professor, along with an impressive resume. When the university rejected him, he was naturally disappointed. This was his "plan" for the post-college transition. But, as we've talked about time after time in our house, not all things go as planned. Sam and I let him sit with his disappointment. And rather than stew in the rejection and shame of not getting accepted or realizing his goal, he pivoted and held his head up. He did not have a plan B worked out, but he had confidence that another path would materialize if he approached it with openness and resilience.

The most important lesson we've taught our kids is how to take what they learned from failing and use it to get better and move forward. It's really what separates the leaders from the followers—this ability to dust yourself off, learn from what went wrong, and jump back in. We've seen each of them develop this skill in their own way, and it's been humbling to watch.

Some of our proudest moments as parents haven't been when our children succeeded, but rather watching how they responded to adversity. These moments of resilience have shaped their leadership styles more profoundly than any big achievement ever could.

THE LEADERSHIP LEGACY

As our children have grown, I've seen them develop their own leadership styles, building on the foundation we provided but expressing their unique strengths. Declan's creativity, Hank's empathy, and Ash's balanced thinking all represent different facets of effective leadership. By giving them the space to develop these qualities in their own ways while providing guidance based on experience, I have watched them grow into thoughtful, capable individuals ready to lead in their own right.

The progression in leadership—both in business and parenting—is to move from dictating to challenging, putting children in positions where they can make choices and learn from them. The power to choose, to try, adjust, fail, and learn is perhaps the greatest gift we can give anyone.

What I've learned through this journey is that leadership isn't something we bestow on our children—it's something we unlock within them. Each of our children had innate qualities that, when nurtured and encouraged, blossomed into their own unique leadership styles. My role wasn't to create carbon copies of myself, but instead to help them recognize and develop their authentic leadership voices.

LEADERSHIP ISN'T SOMETHING WE BESTOW ON OUR CHILDREN— IT'S SOMETHING WE UNLOCK WITHIN THEM.

Perhaps the most rewarding aspect of this journey has been watching how my kids' leadership styles have influenced me in return. Declan's creativity has pushed me to think more innovatively. Hank's natural empathy has reminded me of the human element in every business decision. And Ashleigh's ability to balance pragmatism with emotional intelligence has shown me how powerful that combination can be.

In the end, raising future leaders isn't about teaching our children to follow in our footsteps—it's about giving them the confidence to forge their own paths while carrying forward the values and principles that truly matter. And in doing so, we often find that they become our greatest teachers.

LESSONS LEARNED

- **MODEL WHAT MATTERS—**
  Children absorb what they observe far more than what they're told. My most successful leadership transfers happened not in formal teaching moments, but when I simply included them in my world and let them watch how I handled challenges.

- **STRUCTURE CREATES FREEDOM—**
  Clear boundaries in childhood build confidence for independent decision-making later. The rules and consequences we established early gave our kids the security to exercise autonomy as they grew.

- **RECOGNIZE AND NURTURE DIFFERENT LEADERSHIP STYLES—**
  Some lead through creativity and vision (Declan), others through empathy and inclusion (Hank), and still others through practical problem-solving and emotional intelligence (Ashleigh). None is superior—all are necessary.

- **BEGIN WITH THE END IN MIND, BUT EMBRACE DETOURS—**
  Strategic thinking is valuable, but equally important is the flexibility to adjust when circumstances change, or opportunities arise that weren't part of the original plan.

- **TRUST PRECEDES ACHIEVEMENT—**
  When we trusted our children to rise to occasions, they almost always did. The same principle applies in business—people tend to perform at the level of expectation we set for them.

- **LET NATURAL CONSEQUENCES TEACH—**
  Some of the most powerful leadership lessons for our children came not from our instruction but from experiencing the natural outcomes of their choices.

- **LEADERSHIP DEVELOPMENT IS RECIPROCAL—**
  While we shape our children's leadership abilities, their unique perspectives and talents inevitably reshape our own leadership approach if we remain open to learning.

QUESTIONS FOR REFLECTION

1. How can you intentionally include your children in your professional world in age-appropriate ways?

   _____

   _____

   _____

2. What leadership qualities do you see naturally emerging in your children, and how can you create opportunities for these qualities to develop further?

   _____

   _____

   _____

3. How do you balance providing structure with encouraging autonomy as your children grow?

   _____

   _____

   _____

4. In what ways have you helped your children "begin with the end in mind" when approaching goals or challenges?

   _____
   _____
   _____

5. What leadership lessons from your career have been most valuable in your parenting approach?

   _____
   _____
   _____

6. How do you respond when your children fail or make mistakes? Do you use these moments as opportunities for leadership development?

   _____
   _____
   _____

7. When was the last time you learned something about leadership from your child? What was it, and how did it affect you?

   _____

   _____

   _____

8. How do you communicate and demonstrate your values consistently, both in words and actions?

   _____

   _____

   _____

9. What experiences have you intentionally created or encouraged that might build leadership capacity in your children?

   _____

   _____

   _____

10. How do you balance protecting your children from unnecessary hardship while allowing them to experience the challenges necessary for growth?

_____

_____

_____

RAISING FUTURE LEADERS ISN'T ABOUT TEACHING OUR CHILDREN TO FOLLOW IN OUR FOOTSTEPS—IT'S ABOUT GIVING THEM THE CONFIDENCE TO FORGE THEIR OWN PATHS WHILE CARRYING FORWARD THE VALUES AND PRINCIPLES THAT TRULY MATTER.

s e v e n t e e n

BUILDING OUR FAMILY CULTURE

"The most important work you will ever do will be within the walls of your own home."

HAROLD B. LEE

THE POWER OF INTENTION

People often ask how we managed to stay connected as a family while juggling demanding careers and raising three kids. *"You all genuinely seem to love being together—and your kids are so close. How did you do it?"*

I smile because the truth is—we didn't just get lucky. We didn't wing it. We designed it. Intentionally, thoughtfully, and with a lot of trial and error. What people see now is the result of years of small choices that added up to something big.

Here are ten intentional rules and traditions that shaped our family culture:

1. NO PHONES AT DINNER

We knew from a young age that we needed to model the behavior we expected. If we wanted our kids to be present, we had to be present, too. So from the moment they were old enough to have phones, we set a simple rule that everyone followed: no phones at dinner—whether at home or in restaurants.

When they were little, and we'd go out to eat, we'd lock all our phones in the car. Barring some urgent circumstance, we can all live without our phones for 45 minutes. Those device-free meals became sacred spaces for real connection.

I remember one vacation several years ago—we were seated near another family, all glued to their screens. No one was talking. No one was even looking up. Our kids noticed it, too. "That looks terrible," one of them said. "Let's not be that family." That moment stuck with us.

We still reinforce it today, all five of us, because it's so easy to slip back into distraction. During Hank's graduation weekend, we found ourselves reminding Declan, after she took her usual photos of every meal, to put the phone away.

Our time together is precious. And when we're fully present with one another, the conversation flows, the laughter comes easily, and the bonds grow deeper. No photo or text can replace that.

2. NEVER MISS THE BIG MOMENTS

While my executive role meant I couldn't be a regular classroom mom, I made it a priority to never miss the big stuff. Birthdays, class presentations, talent shows, culture projects—those were non-negotiables.

I had an incredible assistant, Jennifer, who understood just how much those moments mattered. As a mom herself, she knew the weight of a child scanning the audience, hoping to see their parent. She made sure those dates were on my calendar well in advance—and, just as importantly, she fiercely protected them. No meeting, no call, no travel. Jennifer was my gatekeeper, and because of her, I showed up for more than just the obvious milestones.

It wasn't just birthdays. It was the "culture project" where Hank presented about his Irish grandparents. The talent show where Declan rode her unicycle on stage for the first time. The class party where Ash decorated her very own "birthday body" in real-time (see Sam's story in the appendix).

Those were not just calendar events—they were the moments that mattered most. And over time, they became the ones my kids remembered, too.

3. (ALMOST) NO SLEEPOVERS

As a working mom with little kids, weekends were precious. I'd spend the week at work—or on a trip to NYC for market—and the last thing I wanted was over-tired kids after a sleepover or a house full of extra children the next morning.

Some parents thought we were too strict, but preserving our family's rhythm mattered more to us than following the usual social script.

When the pressure mounted and the kids really wanted to go to a sleepover, we found a compromise: stay late—sometimes even until 11 p.m.—and we'd come to pick you up. You'd sleep in your own bed, and we'd drop you back in the morning for breakfast. It wasn't perfect, but it worked. Nine times out of ten, that was enough.

We held firm on the rules that truly mattered, but if it wasn't the end of the world, we looked for ways to compromise. In doing so, our kids learned that some things are non-negotiable, while others require flexibility. It was an important life lesson: knowing when to stand your ground and when to seek a solution that works for everyone without losing your voice or rolling over.

It will be interesting to see how they handle sleepovers when they have kids of their own. My guess? They'll set the same boundaries we did—maybe with a few tweaks of their own—and

> WE HELD FIRM ON RULES THAT TRULY MATTERED, BUT IF IT WASN'T THE END OF THE WORLD, WE LOOKED FOR WAYS TO COMPROMISE.

realize that sometimes, the rules you once resisted are the ones that end up making the most sense.

4. THEIR PATH, NOT OURS

It would have been easy for me to sign the kids up for year-round swimming and push them to follow in my footsteps. Or for Sam to enroll Hank in year-round soccer or basketball—his lifelong passion, and something he'd still play today if he could.

Instead, we took a more considered approach to our kids' activities and achievements. We encouraged them to stay active and involved, but ultimately let them choose their own paths.

Of course, they did summer swim team—for a few good reasons. It was community, it was fun, and it was tradition. I did it growing up and wanted them to have the same experience: running around at swim meets, eating Jell-O straight from the box, playing with friends on warm summer nights. It was also a safety thing—we live on an island, and strong swimming skills were imperative.

But when they each decided they were ready to quit, we let them. I would have loved to see them continue, but that wasn't the point. It wasn't about living out my dreams. It was about letting them find their own.

And they did. Hank and Ashleigh found their passion in lacrosse (both played club lacrosse at the University of Texas). Declan took to swimming and running. They're all still active and enjoy fitness to this day—but they also developed other interests that may not have had room to grow in a schedule packed with year-round select sports.

Reading, travel, cooking—these became part of their lives because we prioritized downtime, family time, and real vacations over constant competition. They weren't chasing our dreams. They were building their own.

5. OURS, NOT MINE

When I was at Nordstrom, even though my name was on the paychecks, we never saw it as "my money" or "my success." Everything was ours—the achievements, the setbacks, the financial decisions. This wasn't just about money; it was about honoring our partnership and recognizing that Sam's role at home made my career possible.

I remember one year when I got a big bonus, and we took a quick trip down to Los Angeles. One of our first stops on the way to Malibu was a jewelry store to buy Sam a watch he had been eyeing for years. It wasn't about the watch—it was about acknowledging everything he made possible behind the scenes and celebrating what we had both accomplished.

Another time, after a particularly demanding stretch at work, he surprised me with a special trip he had secretly planned. That's how we celebrated: in ways that honored both of us.

Often, the money-maker controls the spending. Not in our case. Every financial decision—from vacations to home purchases to charitable giving—was made together. We didn't keep score. We shared the wins, the work, and the rewards—because success only felt real when it was ours, not mine.

6. INTIMACY ISN'T OPTIONAL

Prioritizing intimacy isn't selfish; it's essential to a stable family foundation. Consistent emotional and physical intimacy allowed us to parent with unity, clarity, and love. For us, this was protected by "Tune-Up Tuesdays" (I'll let you use your imagination). This has kept our marriage from falling into autopilot and has maintained our connection as strong and fun today as when we first began.

7. GIVE THE BENEFIT OF THE DOUBT

This wasn't something we nailed from the start. In fact, it took more than a few knock-down, drag-out discussions for us to get here. In the early years, I often came home from a long work trip or late night at the office and zeroed in on everything that wasn't done—laundry piles, dishes in the sink, toys all over the floor. My first instinct was to criticize. I was exhausted, overwhelmed, and honestly, pretty unfair.

But over time, I realized something had to give—and it wasn't going to be our relationship. I decided to change my tune. I had to trust that Sam was doing his best, even if it didn't look like my version of "done." That shift didn't happen overnight, but it changed everything.

Instead of keeping score or questioning each other's effort, we started defaulting to trust. We recognized that the division of labor in our home wouldn't always be 50/50, but it would be fair—and grounded in mutual respect. If the house wasn't perfectly clean or one of us missed bedtime for work, we gave each other grace instead of criticism.

It was a game-changer—not just for us, but for our kids. They saw how we handled the tension and learned to treat each other with the same respect and support. Giving the benefit of the doubt became one of the quietest but most powerful values we passed on to them.

8. MAKE US PROUD

When the kids reached middle school, we introduced them to the idea of *"The Chapin Brand."* It was a bit tongue-in-cheek, but we felt they were old enough to start thinking beyond their individual actions—to understand that how they showed up reflected not just on them, but on our whole family, and all of our reputations.

The concept was simple. It wasn't about status—it was about integrity. *"Make us proud, make good decisions, and treat everyone with kindness and respect"* became our family mantra. (Or, as our Team 17 dad more succinctly put it to his kids: No cops. No babies.)

Whether they were at a high school football game, in the lunchroom, or picking teams during P.E., we reminded them to be the kind of person who includes others. When in doubt, err on the side of the invite. Be the person who notices someone standing alone and makes them feel like they belong.

I'll never forget hosting one of Hank's "after" parties following a school dance. He casually mentioned that 24 kids were coming over... which quickly turned into 32. "I couldn't say no," he shrugged. "They didn't have anywhere else to go." Did I want a bigger group of teenagers at our house until midnight? Not particularly. But I wasn't about to say no. He was being inclusive, and I was proud of him for that.

Or the time Declan said a "couple" of teammates might stop by after swim practice—and 70 girls with wet hair and sweatpants showed up at our door. It was not the first time, and thankfully, I'd anticipated the food order.

No matter what, the message was clear: look people in the eye, treat everyone with the respect they deserve, and don't be an asshole. *Make us proud.*

And they did. And still do today.

Now, as young adults, that mindset shows up in how they treat roommates, lead teams, navigate friendships, and advocate for others. Their "brand" isn't something they

WHEN YOU LEAD WITH INTEGRITY EARLY ON, THE REST OF THE BEHAVIORS TEND TO FOLLOW.

perform—it's who they are. Turns out, when you lead with integrity early on, the rest of the behaviors tend to follow.

9. CHOOSE YOUR TRIBE WISELY

We were fortunate to find kindred spirits in two other families who shared our values. Together, we called ourselves *Team 17*—eleven kids between three families, all fiercely dedicated to each other and to the family unit. Our families became more than friends; they became a living, breathing example that our approach to parenting, partnership, and presence could work.

We spent countless summer weekends together at one family's beach house, where Sunday often turned into Monday because no one wanted the fun to end. I vividly remember the very early Monday morning drives with one of the husbands, both of us rushing back for work, the kids still at the house skipping swim practice. Our hearts were full—never once regretting those extra hours around the barbecue, kids piled into the bunk room, or gathered by the bonfire—chatting, laughing, and singing along as Sam played his guitar late into the night.

There was even a time when a barista at the local café assumed Sam and one of the other moms were a couple with six kids in tow. They didn't correct her—they just smiled and ordered another round of hot chocolates for "their kids." That moment captured the essence of what we'd built: a community where the lines between "yours" and "mine" had blurred into *ours*.

Our kids grew up more like siblings than friends, and we co-parented all eleven of them—cheering at games, navigating middle school drama, and tagging in for carpools and tough conversations. We became each other's greatest support system through all of life's highs and lows.

It wasn't just shared values—it was shared life. And that made all the difference.

10. PARENTS AT THE CENTER

From Sam's parents, we learned one of the most valuable lessons long before it even became our reality: Parents should be the center of the family universe, with the kids orbiting around that solid core. If we stayed strong and united, nothing could disrupt our family's bond.

It sounds simple, but it wasn't always easy. When the kids were little, keeping our relationship front and center took intention and effort. Between work, school events, swim meets, and sick days, even squeezing in a date night—or a short weekend away—felt like a luxury. But we always knew the long game was about more than just surviving those busy years. It was about building something that would outlast them.

Now, in the season we're in—empty nesting—we've fiercely refocused on *us*. After years of full-time parenting, carpools, college visits, and chaos, we've reclaimed our time and energy for each other. We take our own extended vacations, enjoy everyday rituals together, and prioritize our connection without apology. The kids see it, they respect it, and—most of the time—they don't infringe on it.

A recent favorite: while all three kids went skiing together for spring break, Sam and I jetted off to the Caribbean—just the two of us. When we all reunited, they scrolled through our camera roll and laughed, saying we had a more fun spring break than they did. (They weren't wrong.)

It's like putting Miracle-Gro® on our relationship—and as we continue to grow, so do they. When we're united, strong, and undivided, our whole family thrives. Honestly, *us having fun* is their favorite kind of stability. And that's the greatest gift we could give them.

CONCLUSION

Being present was the key to all these rules. Whether in the house, at a game, or during a simple conversation, we were present and expected the kids to be present, too. And they definitely picked up on that. Even when kids act like they're not paying attention, they are. And it matters.

Just last month, all three kids were home for dinner. No phones. Just stories, teasing, and laughter. It hit me like a wave—they're here because they want to be. That's the legacy I care most about.

Some might call our approach old-fashioned or overly structured. But watching our children grow into adults who still choose to spend time with us—and with each other—makes me believe we got something right.

In the end, isn't that what family culture is really about?

Maybe your family's culture will look different. But the magic is in the *choosing*—and the showing up. Start small, stay present, and build what matters most.

LESSONS LEARNED

- INTENTIONALITY—
  Things that matter don't happen by chance. Every tradition, rule, and practice we established took conscious effort and consistent reinforcement. While it was often easier to go with the flow of modern family life, standing firm in our intentions helped shape the family unit we truly wanted.

- BOUNDARIES—
  Clear family rules and expectations didn't restrict us—they freed us. Our "no phones at dinner" policy allowed for real connection. The "almost no sleepovers" rule preserved our weekend rhythm. Boundaries like these removed the constant case-by-case negotiations and created a sense of stability for everyone.

- **TRUST—**
  Our family unit was built on mutual trust between Sam and me. By giving each other the benefit of the doubt and recognizing all contributions—both financial and non-financial—we laid a solid foundation. That example taught our children what true partnership and respect look like.

- **PRESENCE—**
  Being engaged—whether at a little league game, a class presentation, or a weeknight dinner—mattered more than anything overly orchestrated. Our presence spoke louder than any grand gesture.

- **COMMUNITY—**
  Spending time with like-minded families (our "Team 17") validated our choices and gave our children a broader circle of support. These relationships reminded us that while every family is different, sharing core values with others only strengthens your own.

- **INVESTMENT—**
  Building family culture is a long game. There were days we wondered if our efforts were making a

> **BUILDING FAMILY CULTURE IS A LONG GAME.**

difference. But now, watching our grown children stay close, carry our values, and choose time together—we know those early investments paid off in ways we never could have predicted.

QUESTIONS FOR REFLECTION

1. What unwritten rules or traditions currently shape your family's culture? Which ones feel meaningful, and which might be ready for a reset?

   _____

   _____

   _____

2. What are your "non-negotiables" in family life—the values or practices you're unwilling to compromise on, and why?

   _____

   _____

   _____

3. Who makes up your "tribe"? How do the people who support and align with your family values influence your journey?

4. How do you balance career demands with being present at home? What moments feel truly *unmissable*, and how do you protect them?

5. What does your version of a "family brand" look like? What values, behaviors, or messages do you want associated with your family name?

6. How do you define success in your family life? What matters most—beyond achievements or appearances?

eighteen

PROOF OF CONCEPT

"You know it worked when your kids become your legacy—not because they followed your footsteps, but because they found their own with the values you gave them."

LORETTA SOFFE

IN THEIR OWN WORDS

By now, you've read the stories—of role reversal, career leaps, messy mornings, controlled chaos ... and intentional living. I've shared the values that shaped our choices: connection over convention, growth over perfection, experiences over things, and family first—always.

It's one thing to talk about values—it's another to live them. This is where that gets real.

Our children are now thriving young adults—living proof that balance, as traditionally defined, isn't just overrated. It's bullshit.

We weren't rigid, but we thrived on structure. I like to think I kept things moving, but Sam was the one who kept it humming—day in and day out. He developed the systems and standards that grounded our home, and together, we created a rhythm and momentum that made it all work.

Together, we raised not just good kids, but compassionate, creative, driven, and self-aware humans. I wanted them to share what it was really like to grow up in a house where love came first, roles were reimagined, and success was defined on our terms.

I asked my editor to interview each of our kids and encouraged them to answer freely—in their own words, in their own voices. As a parent, reading their responses made me laugh out loud and brought me to tears. More than anything, it was deeply affirming and profoundly heartwarming. Their maturity, self-awareness, and emotional insight moved me—not because I was surprised (I've always known those qualities were there), but because hearing them express their values so clearly is a feeling that's hard to put into words. If you're a parent to older "kids," you understand. And if you're not there yet—trust me, it's coming.

It's what drives me to help other mothers feel that same sense of connection, intention, and joy—because I know how hard it is to hold it all and how deeply rewarding it can be when you do.

I want women to know you can have both—a career you love and a family that thrives. And I want to encourage couples to truly partner with each other to get clear on what matters most, to set priorities that reflect their values, and to create the kind of support that makes raising strong, grounded, connected kids not just possible—but joyful.

And now, without further ado, here are five key takeaways from each kid's interview.

THE LITTLE WITNESS
THROUGH THE EYES OF ASHLEIGH

1. **Our family structure felt normal, even if others found it unusual.**

   I grew up fully accustomed to having my dad as the primary caregiver. While some of my friends found it unusual that my dad was the one showing up at preschool or organizing playdates, I never saw it as strange. To me, it was simply the way things were, and I never felt like my dad fell short compared to other moms.

2. **Discipline and independence are my core values because my parents instilled them in me.**

My dad had high expectations of us, especially around our behavior, honesty, and responsibility. We couldn't get away with anything, which I hated as a kid, but I appreciate it now. Our home was highly structured. My dad was strict and never flinched in a battle of wills, but this has made me more independent, confident, and probably more resilient than many of my peers. They still influence how I show up—how I treat people, take responsibility, and stay motivated in school and life.

3. **I enjoy a deep and meaningful relationship with both parents. That's rare.**

In my early years, I had a particularly close bond with my dad. We had a lot of similar interests, and we just got to spend a lot of time together. Few kids get to experience this, and I feel lucky. Then, during my teenage years, as I matured, the roles reversed again. Dad went back to a career, and Mom came home (got fired). So, I had the opportunity to spend quality time with her, and our relationship deepened as a result. Today, I feel equally comfortable talking to either parent about things. If I want emotional support, I'm going to Mom. She'll cry it out with me. But if I need practical advice that points me toward mature decisions, I'm going to my dad. Honestly, I need both angles.

4. I learned powerful lessons about gender roles, prioritizing experiences, and staying flexible.

Watching my parents create a nontraditional family structure taught me that gender roles in parenting should be flexible and based on what works best for the family. I admire my dad for stepping into that role with such confidence—he's raised the bar for what I'll expect in a future spouse. I hope to recreate many aspects of my childhood in my own family one day, especially the mutual support and open-mindedness my parents modeled.

And more than anything, I want to give my future family the same gift mine gave me: experiences over things. The way my parents prioritized travel, adventure, and quality time made me curious about the world and helped me stay grounded in what really matters. It also created a special bond with my siblings from as early as I can remember—and it's the reason we're best friends today. That perspective will stay with me for life.

5. My parents set me up for success by making their expectations clear—without putting on pressure.

Growing up, it was always clear that we were expected to succeed—especially in school. But it never felt like pressure. My parents set high standards around how we behaved, how hard we worked, and how we treated others, but those expectations came from a place of belief in us, not control.

That kind of clarity gave me a solid foundation. I picked up on those values early, and they've just become part of who I am. I'm naturally driven—I like putting in the work and doing things well, not because anyone's pushing me, but because it matters to me. I do well in school, and I know the confidence I feel in college—and in whatever comes next—is 100% shaped by how I was raised.

MIDDLE SEAT, FRONT ROW
HANK'S TAKE

1. **Nontraditional roles are normal.**

I never saw our family's structure as unusual. Dad being our primary caregiver felt completely natural to me. What kid even thinks about who is taking care of them and if it is weird or not? I never noticed it was different from my friends unless someone else pointed it out. But watching my mom be an executive and my dad be a confident man who happened to take care of us helped shape my open-minded view on gender roles later in life. I see women as smart, caring, and capable of succeeding at anything they choose to do. I expect men to respect women in this way, and I am sometimes surprised when they don't.

2. **My dad's consistent presence in my childhood gave me a foundation of stability.**

   Looking back, I've come to really appreciate how much stability and structure came from having my dad around every day. There was something grounding about his routines—whether it was him making us breakfast every single morning, driving us to school, or playing his guitar in the living room at night. Those small, consistent moments added up to something much bigger: a deep sense of safety, connection, and trust.

   He wasn't just around—he was really present. He set the pace for our days, kept things on track, and had this calm energy that made everything feel manageable, even during the chaos of school mornings or whatever meltdown was happening that day. Having a dad who showed up every single day—with structure, sarcasm, and support—definitely shaped how I think about fatherhood and being a good partner someday. It set the bar in a way I probably didn't realize until I got older.

3. **Since we weren't allowed to run wild, I guess we learned how to stand firm.**

   My dad was definitely the stricter parent. He kept us on a tight leash—especially in the mornings, during school routines, and at bedtime. Zero tolerance. (I was going to tell the grape story here, but now it's in the appendix, so ... yeah.)

Mom wasn't nearly as rigid, but she didn't really need to be. Dad already had that role locked down. She brought a different kind of energy—more flexible, more emotional, more about talking things through. She was softer, less strict, and definitely more likely to make things fun instead of structured. She was the one who'd turn a stressful moment into a joke or a dance party, who'd let us off the hook sometimes, or be ready with a hug when that's what we really needed.

It was a solid balance. When Dad laid down the law, Mom gave us space to process it. When one of us needed empathy or a shift in perspective, she was the one we went to. Looking back, I don't regret the structure at all. It taught me discipline, accountability, and a strong work ethic early on—and those values are a huge part of who I am now. I'm grateful they played different roles that worked together so well.

4. Having traditional values but fluid gender roles lived out with mutual respect made me adaptable.

We had a really traditional family, even though it was a reversed-gender role household. This has made the concept of shared or alternative parenting roles approachable and realistic. I'm not sure how I'll handle it yet, but I believe that family dynamics should be flexible and based on what works in each unique situation—not constrained by tradition.

5. **My parents are a lasting influence on my interests and goals.**

   I just graduated from college, and my path in economics was entirely interest-driven. My mom's career in retail sparked my curiosity about the business world and gave me an early appreciation for creativity and brand-building. But it was the dynamic between both of my parents—the way they approached career, family, and everything in between—that really shaped me. Their example helped me develop ambition, adaptability, and a real appreciation for living a full, well-rounded life. Honestly, both my parents and my siblings have played a huge role in shaping who I am and what I want going forward.

THE COMPASS POINTS EVERYWHERE
A CONVERSATION WITH DECLAN
(THE FAMILY'S WILD SOUL)

1. **A nontraditional setup was empowering for a young girl.**

   Growing up with a working mom and a stay-at-home dad never felt strange to me. If anything, it felt empowering. I never felt the need to explain it—maybe people were curious, but I was so secure in who I was and how I was raised that I didn't think twice about it.

Being raised by a structured, direct, and deeply present dad gave me confidence, courage, and emotional resilience. His no-nonsense parenting style taught me discipline, how to cope, and how to face the world head-on.

And my mom? She was a boss. Literally. Watching her step off a corporate jet in heels left a lasting impression. She showed me—without ever having to say it—that women can do anything. Those lessons, from both of them, are still shaping who I am today.

2. **Discipline, routine, and emotional grounding were gifts in disguise.**

Our daily life was structured and consistent. We had simple meals (often the same thing every day), strict bedtimes, and repeated routines—which, in hindsight, offered stability and freed up mental space for creativity and intellectual growth. The meals weren't exactly nutritious—they were more about what was easy to prep and what we'd actually eat. Fishy crackers, frozen waffles, bagels with cream cheese, and Oreos were basically food groups. But my parents didn't stress about it. They knew we'd outgrow that phase eventually—and we did. What mattered more was the rhythm and consistency, and looking back, I can see how much that structure helped us feel safe and free to grow.

In my early years, I often clashed with my dad, but looking back, I can now appreciate that his strictness (discipline) and consistency were one of the greatest gifts he could give us. His red-pen edits on my school papers and his no-nonsense attitude toward behavior have shaped me into someone who values hard work, reliability, and grit.

3. **Because gender roles were redefined in our home, it changed my perspective permanently.**

   Having a strong, supportive father at home and a powerful, successful mother at work shattered all the traditional gender role expectations. I never once saw being a girl as limiting. The model my parents lived out, where the man supported the woman's career and still maintained his own intellectual and personal growth, deeply influenced how I view relationships, work-life balance, and what I look for in a partner.

4. **Prioritizing strong family bonds and shared experiences was the right call.**

   Even with my mom's demanding career and my dad managing the day-to-day of our home life, family was always the top priority. We had regular dinners around the table, monthly get-togethers with friends, tech-light routines, and travel that created lasting memories. Those rhythms gave us a sense of connection that's stayed with me into adulthood.

My family are still the people I most want to be with. I'm super close with my parents, and my siblings are truly my best friends. I've even chosen a career path that lets me stay close to them. The values I hold—community, hospitality, humility—all come from the intentional, experience-rich way my parents raised us.

5. **The long game pays off.**

Watching my dad put his career on pause—but not completely on hold—instilled lessons in delayed gratification, personal growth, and an entrepreneurial spirit. He never stopped learning or preparing for the next chapter, and now, years later, I see him thriving in a new professional phase of his life.

After her successful career with Nordstrom, my mom had more time and flexibility to be there for us—but she never stopped being driven. She started her own consulting business and kept pushing herself, growing, and finding new ways to lead. Watching her do that while still being so present at home made a big impression on me. I've always looked up to both of my parents, but in different ways—and I'm incredibly proud of who they are and what they've built together.

They prioritized their marriage, which gave us a loving, stable environment. They modeled patience, resilience, and long-term vision. Today, my own goals center around living with intention, exploring faith, maintaining my autonomy, doing meaningful work, and building a family that mirrors the deep bonds and values I grew up with.

MORE THAN SIBLINGS— BEST FRIENDS

Our kids didn't just grow up under the same roof—they grew up *together*. We emphasized shared experiences: family dinners, travel, game nights, and traditions like ski weekends in our RV and holiday rituals. Sure, they fought (over everything from who got shotgun to whose turn it was to unload the dishwasher), but underneath it all, we taught them to respect each other, to apologize, and to cheer each other on. Today, they are each other's confidants, biggest fans, and favorite travel companions. Of everything we built, their closeness as siblings is what brings us the most joy.

PROOF OF CONCEPT

That's what this chapter is really about. Not just that we made unconventional choices—but that those choices produced something lasting. We raised three very different kids, each with their own voice, their own path, and their own perspective. And yet, the common thread in all of them is clear: love, loyalty, resilience, confidence, and clarity. Not because we got it all right, but because we kept showing up—with intention, with humor, and with each other. This is the long game. And the results speak for themselves.

If we had chased "balance," we might have missed everything. But by staying focused—first on each other, then on our kids, and always on our values—we created something far richer: a family culture that lasts.

They say the truest test of a life well-lived is not just in what you accomplish but in what you pass on. These reflections—from Ashleigh, Hank, and Declan—are our proof of concept. That clear expectations and steady support matter more than rigid rules. That love and leadership can live under the same roof. And that when you raise your family with clarity, intention, and a good sense of humor, something extraordinary happens: they carry it forward.

FOR THE PARENTS READING THIS

You don't have to do it the way everyone else is doing it. Define success on your own terms. Build your life around your values—not someone else's expectations. Your kids are watching how you live, not just what you say.

There's no one "right" way—only what's right for *your* family. Don't be afraid to flip the script if it brings you closer to what truly matters.

Balance is bullshit. Presence, intention, and love—that's what lasts. In the end, it's not about doing it all right—it's about showing up, again and again.

QUESTIONS FOR REFLECTION

1. What values do you hope your children will grow up with? How are you beginning to model those—intentionally or not—in your everyday life?

   _____

   _____

   _____

2. How are you and your partner approaching roles at home and in your careers? What messages might those choices send about partnership, parenting, and possibility?

   _____

   _____

   _____

3. When you imagine your child as a young adult, what qualities do you hope they'll have? What choices can you make now to help lay that foundation?

   _____

   _____

   _____

4. How can you build a home where connection, shared experiences, and emotional resilience matter more than perfection or performance?

_____

_____

_____

5. What does *success* look like for your family—not just on paper, but in real life? What would it mean to thrive together?

_____

_____

_____

n i n e t e e n

THE LIFE YOU CHOOSE

BECAUSE BALANCE WAS NEVER THE POINT

"And when you get the choice to sit it out or dance—I hope you'll dance."

LEE ANN WOMACK

DEAR DECLAN, HANK, AND ASHLEIGH—
AND ALL WHO HAVE READ THIS BOOK,

One day, you'll look back on your own life—on the choices you made, the dreams you chased, the family you built—and you'll ask yourself: "Did I live it fully? Did I love deeply? Did I stay true to who I am?"

BALANCE IS BULLSHIT

I hope that this book gives you part of that answer.

It's not a manual; it's a message. A message about grit and grace, about choosing love over ego, purpose over pressure, and faith over fear. It's about the life your dad and I built—imperfect, unconventional, and entirely our own—and the lessons we learned along the way.

Because here's the truth: **BALANCE IS BULLSHIT.**

The secret was never about doing it all. It was about believing—in myself, in the people I love, and in the life we were determined to build. It is the belief that we could write our own script. Belief that partnership didn't have to fit a mold. And the belief that love—real love—meant showing up, honoring our differences, supporting each other's strengths, and never apologizing for making bold choices.

I didn't write this book as a roadmap. I wrote it as a reminder. There's no one right path. There's just "your" path—and it's worth walking with intention, grace, and courage.

You've heard the full, messy truth—about my firing, our family, my faith, our failures, and everything in between. Not because I wanted to be admired but because I wanted you to feel seen. I wanted you to know that your own story, in all its complexity, is worthy, too.

Because your story deserves to be lived—and told.

You watched Daddy and I trade places. While I climbed the corporate ladder, your dad became the steady presence at home. It wasn't traditional. It wasn't trendy. It was simply what worked for us. That decision—countercultural at the time—wasn't about making a point. It was about sacrifice and building a life anchored in trust and mutual respect.

And marriage? It was never about keeping score—it was about staying connected. Ours was built on coins, compromise, and commitment. In the early days, we literally emptied a change jar to buy groceries. But more than the money, what mattered was the mindset: we were in it together.

We made every major decision—from parenting to career moves to household duties—as a team. We raised kids in tandem, shifted roles when life required it, and supported each other's ambitions without keeping tabs. It didn't look traditional. And it certainly wasn't perfect. But it was "ours"—built on a deep respect for one another's strengths.

We didn't wait for permission. We didn't follow a script. We wrote our own—and kept rewriting it as life evolved.

And when life knocked me flat—when I walked out of that office with a box in hand and no job title left to hide behind—I chose grace. I didn't collapse. I stood tall. I walked away with my head held high and, more importantly, with clarity. Because sometimes, when things are falling apart, they're actually falling into place.

Before any of that, I learned to swim in cold water, mostly on really early, dark mornings. My Irish roots taught me that conditions don't need to be perfect for you to begin. You just dive in. You stay grateful. You work hard. And when you fall down, and you will often, "You get back up and begin again" as Brene Brown so eloquently said.

Resilience isn't something you're born with—it's something you build. Practice by practice. Choice by choice. One hard moment at a time.

And motherhood? That's the deepest end. Nothing—not even corporate life—tests your limits like becoming a mother. The postpartum depression I experienced after Ash was born was humbling. I thought I could outwork it or positive-think my way through it. But healing came through vulnerability, support, and time. And it shaped me into a more compassionate and real version of myself.

You didn't need a perfect mom—you just needed me to show up. And I did. Not flawlessly, but faithfully. With love and all my heart—even on the hardest days. Of all the things I've done, becoming your mom stretched me the most, and it, without a doubt, is what I am most proud of.

Leadership didn't start in the boardroom—it started at home. It didn't come with a title or a spotlight, but in the everyday moments: being present, setting expectations, and building a family rooted in love and loyalty. We weren't trying to raise prodigies. We were raising kind, strong, capable humans who knew who they were and how to treat others. And the truth is, while we were busy teaching you, you were quietly shaping us, too.

To anyone else reading this—especially the women out there trying to do it all, be it all, hold it all together—I hope you'll take this letter as a reminder: you don't have to do it perfectly. Perfection was never the goal. You just have to do it in a way that feels true to who you are. Let go of the noise, the pressure, the comparison. What matters most isn't how it looks—it's how it feels. If it feels right in your soul and sits well in your spirit, you're already doing it right.

> WOMEN TRY TO DO IT ALL, BE IT ALL, AND HOLD IT ALL TOGETHER—BUT PERFECTION ISN'T THE GOAL. DO WHAT FEELS RIGHT IN YOUR SOUL AND SITS WELL IN YOUR SPIRIT.

We were lucky to have such strong examples. Your grandparents, Steve and Colleen (Dad's parents), showed us what it looks like to love generously, laugh often, and show up—over and over again, no matter what. As parents and grandparents, their consistency in our lives and the deep traditions they created became the backdrop for what we hoped to build in our own family. Their love didn't just guide us—it's been a steady presence in your lives, too. Never take that for granted—it is precious and rare.

And my parents—your grandparents—shaped me in ways I still feel every day. My mother was a quiet force, the kind of leader who didn't need a title to make things happen. She ran our home with discipline, faith, and fierce love. She taught me how to how to keep things running with grace under pressure, and how to pour into others without losing yourself in the process.

My dad epitomized hard work and quiet sacrifice. He took big risks so we could have opportunities he only dreamed of, and he carried the weight of that responsibility with humility and grace. But as hard as he worked, he also taught me to laugh—to find the joy in everyday moments, to not take life too seriously, and to never, *ever* take your faith for granted.

The love stories, sacrifices, and steady presence of your grandparents—all of it laid the groundwork for the life your dad and I built. We didn't copy it exactly. We made it our own. But the values—faith, family, commitment, showing up even when it's hard—those stayed with us.

And now, they live in you.

So, if you take nothing else from this book, take this:

You don't have to choose between ambition and family.

You don't have to lead like anyone else.

You don't need a title to be a leader.

And you don't have to have it all figured out.

THE LIFE YOU CHOOSE

You just have to be brave enough to begin.

When it's hard—show up anyway.

When it's messy—embrace it.

When love feels ordinary—choose it.

When the path looks different than you imagined—walk it anyway.

Because this is your life. Not your mom's or dad's, not your boss's, and not the version you see on Instagram.

Yours.

So, live it fully.

Live it bravely.

Live it with grit and with grace.

Go and build the life only you were meant to live.

And know this—I'm cheering for you.

Always.

With all my heart,

Mama

BALANCE IS BULLSHIT

GO AND BUILD THE
LIFE YOU WERE
MEANT TO LIVE.

twenty

STORIES FROM SAM

THE NIGHT I LEARNED I DIDN'T "DO" ENOUGH

It is an incontrovertible truth that every married couple has this fight and has it often: Who does more? Who has the harder "job"?

I should start by first acknowledging that Loretta is very appreciative of me. She recognizes the sacrifice I've made and the level of tedium that comes with being a stay-at-home dad. She credits me for helping her thrive in her career and allowing her to enjoy the time she gets with the kids rather than spending it doing errands and chores. She thanks me for handling the logistics of our life, from carpools to grocery shopping, cooking and cleaning, to the endless list of other shit I handle while she keeps me in the lifestyle to which I've grown accustomed.

BALANCE IS BULLSHIT

Can you feel the "but" coming?

(But) there are times when she forgets the challenges of dealing with demanding toddlers all day. Like her confederate working dads, she overlooks the fact that there is often little or no adult interaction, no stimulation, and an overdose of monotony for the parent at home. It seems sometimes she believes the cliché that my days involve watching *Oprah* while munching Bonbons.

Or that I *get* to organize play dates where I *get* to drink coffee and chat with her friends who also *get* to stay home with their kids. Whenever you hear "get to" from your spouse while he or she is describing your day, be ready for the fight about who does more. The times I hear "get to" from Loretta, not surprisingly, tend to follow a stressful day or week at work.

The Night I Learned I Didn't Do Enough occurred after one of those days. She had arrived at the office early, and the day was apparently a shit storm from minute one. We had not communicated all day, and when she walked into the house that evening, she was dismayed by the disarray.

It went something like this:

Loretta comes in the door at 6:30 p.m., looks around, and sees chaos. I liked to think of it as "controlled chaos," but such hair-splitting was moot at that point. Kids were yelling, running all over, and toys were strewn everywhere. The kitchen was a mess.

Loretta: [heavy sigh, frustration written all over face] "Hi."

Me: "Hi. How was work?"

Loretta: "Crazy. Meetings all day. Barely had time to pee," She says in staccato as she heads upstairs to change, taking one last disappointed look at the state of the family room.

Uh oh. I'm pretty sure I know where this night is headed.

I serve dinner, clean up, and the night progresses normally. She keeps her discontent in check until she finally snaps as we're getting ready for bed. Keeping a loose grip on her frustration, she says, "You know, I don't like coming home after working so hard all day and having the house look atrocious."

"Well it was actually pretty clean until about an hour before you got home when I started making dinner while our *three* kids were playing," I say, stressing the large number of kids we have.

"Well ... I shouldn't have to come home and pick up the whole house," she says, playing the martyr card a bit early for my liking.

I am calm. "That's funny because I don't remember asking you to pick up anything," I say with just a pinch of sarcasm. Note: As satisfying as sarcasm can be, it is not a winning strategy in this type of discussion.

Seeing my sarcasm and raising me one pinch more, she says, "What did you *do* all day?" Between the tone and the rhetorical sentence structure, it seemed pretty clear there was not an answer that was going to satisfy her.

What did you do all day? This is a question my working guy friends ask their stay-at-home mom wives. Or at least it's a question my guy friends frequently ask me about their wives because they understand that asking this question directly to their wives will not improve their sex lives. If they do ask it, they only make that mistake once. Loretta would laugh if I attempted to give her the headache treatment, and if she called my bluff, I would fold like a house of cards. So, as a man, my only option is to be angry when that question is asked of me.

I stayed silent, my blood starting to simmer. Maybe it's my training as a trial lawyer, but I can resist being pulled into emotional arguments. As everyone who knows me can attest, I have no problem arguing my position passionately on any subject. I am not conflict-averse. Arguments between husband and wife are obviously different, however, and I try to avoid passionate positions in arguments on days when Loretta has a shitty day at the office.

One thing I never do is bore her with lists or complaints about everything that happened during the day. As I've always said, sometimes the days are easy, and sometimes they're a tedious pain in the ass. I figure the last thing anyone wants to hear after working all day is a big laundry list of the mundane aspects of the at-home parent's day.

I'd heard enough private complaints from guys that they don't enjoy being hit with a barrage of complaints about how challenging the day was because of poopy diapers and errands. That always made sense to me, and I have never once complained in that fashion. Now, don't get me wrong, I've definitely said things like, "Thank God you're home—the kids are driving me crazy!" But even those days, I can count on one hand (not days where the kids drove me crazy, just days I actually complained about it).

So when she asked what I did all day, or rather, when she not-so-subtly accused me of doing nothing, I had a couple of options: fight or write. Being a writer, or possibly just a wuss, I chose the more passive option.

The day, in fact, had been fairly normal. Like usual, it did not involve *Oprah*, Bonbons, or coffee dates. Instead of arguing, I penned out a timesheet very similar to when I worked in private practice at a Seattle law firm and had to account for every six minutes of my time. I took great care to record accurately the minutes, always mindful of my ethical responsibility not to over-bill my client (I was an honest lawyer).

Following is the typed version of the hand-written timesheet I gave to Loretta, without comment, before we went to sleep:

MONDAY

7:00-9:00 a.m.: Breakfast for all 3, make lunches to comply with everyone's individual requests and health concerns, clean up lunch, do dishes

9:00-9:30 a.m.: Walk all 3 to the bus, then drive Ashleigh to pre-school

9:30-10:00 a.m: Go to UPS store to mail packages for you

10:15-11:35 a.m.: Swim

11:35-12:00 p.m.: Pick up Ashleigh, hang out at pre-school, watching her play on those little yellow walking cups with the strings attached

12:00-1:30 p.m.: Go to mall with Ashleigh for lunch, check out a couple of stores for stuff we need; Go to grocery store to pick up photos (photos still not there—third time you sent me for them in last two days); go to health food store for your vitamins

1:30 p.m: Put Ash down for her nap; do remainder of dishes; clean up house; work on bills

2:15 p.m: Hank off bus, walked Declan to Grace's house, came home and played with Hank, more home paperwork

4:20 p.m.: Drove Hank to basketball practice; went to grocery store

4:45 p.m.: Picked up Declan and Grace and took them to soccer practice

- **5:15 p.m.:** Started cooking dinner, all the while watching the kids playing and riding scooters in street; set table for dinner
- **5:45 p.m.:** Picked up Hank after basketball; picked up Declan after soccer
- **6:00 p.m.:** You arrive home
- **6:15 p.m.:** Dish up everyone's dinner, clear everyone's dinner plates, do all dishes, make coffee for morning, make warm cocoas for kids before bed, help put kids to bed
- **9:00 p.m.:** Learn that I didn't "do" enough today.

Okay, so it was a *tad* passive-aggressive.

She read the list, put it on her bedside table, and went to sleep. Needless to say, the *only* thing we did in bed that night was sleep.

To her credit, the next morning, Loretta apologized. She admitted she might have overlooked a few of the things I had done during the day. In response, I pledged to strive for a more peaceful and clean environment when she arrives home from work. We kissed and made up properly. And so it seemed we reached an understanding that would have made Dr. Phil proud.

I know this from watching *Oprah*.

THE GREAT GRAPE STANDOFF

Very often, parenting simply comes down to a battle of wills.

I had never lost such a battle to a toddler, but I had never met an opponent like our son, Hank. When it came to eating and trying anything new, he was intransigent. He would not blink. He would not budge. He was happy to go hungry. He was even picky about kid food; refusing to eat noodles—even mac n' cheese, for Christ's sake—until he was six years old. What kid doesn't eat mac n' cheese?

The noodle issue didn't bother us much because noodles aren't exactly steamed broccoli from a nutritional perspective. It merely presented a challenge when every other kid was being fed mac n' cheese or spaghetti, and our kid had to have some meat product instead. A noodle-free zone we could tolerate, but Hank's refusal to eat most fruits and vegetables was now, belatedly, unacceptable.

I knew we dropped the ball with Hank. We'd done so well with Declan. She ate a ton of different foods, fruits, and vegetables. Her sweet-tooth was her Achilles' Heel. She would practically eat anything upon the threat of withholding the whipped cream on an ice cream sundae.

Hank, on the other hand, could not be bought. He could not be bullied. This would be a good time to cue up the whistling musical theme from the Clint Eastwood classic movie *THE*

GOOD, THE BAD, AND THE UGLY. The standoff that was about to begin was truly a battle of wills.

It was a random weekday morning in February 2006. Loretta was in Los Angeles for work, and I was serving a relatively unhealthy version of breakfast to the kids. Ash was nine months old, strapped into her highchair and eating something soft that was designed not to choke her to death. Hank was about three and a half, sitting in his blue plastic booster seat buckled to a barstool at the kitchen island next to Declan, who had just turned five. They were enjoying some mini-cakes (microwaveable mini pancakes), sausage, and grapes.

To even give "grapes" a billing on the breakfast fare that morning is a bit of a stretch. Hank had *two grapes* on his plastic plate. And, after he and everyone else finished breakfast, there were still two grapes on his plate.

"Hank, you haven't eaten your grapes. You need to eat those, Buddy," I encouraged, smiling.

"I don't like 'em."

"How do you know if you don't like grapes—have you ever eaten grapes?" I said, thinking logic was going to carry the day.

Logic was not in a carrying mood. "Noooo ... I just don't like them," he said.

"Okay, well, you *have* to eat them," I said, this time dispensing with the encouraging tone. "Come on, man, they're good. Just eat 'em!" Right back to the encouraging tone. So much for being tough.

He looked me straight in the eye, strained against the booster seat's little yellow strap that buckled him in, and pushed his plate about a foot further away from him. He said matter-of-factly, "I don't want to."

I think I was actually able to see the period at the end of his sentence as he completed it. We stared at each other, Clint Eastwood style.

I imagine his confidence brimmed because he believed he was on safe ground. Loretta and I are strict disciplinarians when it comes to behavior, but aside from withholding treats, we had not punished the kids for refusing to eat. Hank had been getting away with being a picky eater without much repercussion so, in his mind, he had this battle all but won by missing a future dessert. And he was fine with that.

I, however, was done conceding. This was a direct reflection on me as a parent—especially as the stay-at-home parent. Aside from Loretta, there was simply no one else to blame. Kids would eat doughnuts and French fries all day long if no one was there to force them to eat a variety of foods, both healthy *and* unhealthy. The picky eaters are allowed to be that way because their parents have surrendered (like we did)! These parents feel it is more important for the child to eat *something* than nothing, and they justify their own laziness by suggesting everyone eventually eats better as they grow up, so what if it means special meals now? We prefer restaurants with kids' menus. The excuses pile up like uneaten carrots.

So there I stood, sipping my coffee, staring at Hank, and contemplating how I was going to handle this situation. I saw three kids and three special meals from now until eternity if I continued relenting. I remembered the common sense advice a friend's pediatrician once gave her when she complained her son was unwilling to eat vegetables. Her doctor said, "Don't let him eat anything until he eats his vegetables. And don't worry if he skips the meal; we've never lost a child to starvation that way."

I decided to dig in. Hank was not going to starve, but he *was* going to eat those grapes. And so began what came to be known as The Great Grape Standoff.

> I DECIDED TO DIG IN. HANK WAS NOT GOING TO STARVE, BUT HE *WAS* GOING TO EAT THOSE GRAPES.

"Okay, Hank," I said, grabbing a flower petal-shaped plastic plate from the cabinet, "I'm going to save these grapes for you on this plate, and you're not going to eat anything else today until you eat both of these grapes. Understand?"

"Um-hmm," he said confidently.

I knew I could enforce the fast since I was going to be with him all day. Declan didn't have pre-school, so we ran a few errands before heading home to hang out until lunch. I was ready for lunchtime and round two of the Standoff.

When lunchtime came, I decided to begin the torture early, and I made one of Hank's favorites for Declan and Ash: Grilled cheese sandwiches, apple slices, and fishy crackers. I buckled him into his booster seat and set the plate with the pair of grapes in front of him; then, I served his sisters his favorite lunch.

He sat there ignoring his plate, unfazed by the thought of skipping lunch. After all, he had eaten a full breakfast. Like a boxer who took a few body blows and scored no connections, I realized I was probably going to lose this round.

He casually offered to eat some apple slices instead of grapes, and I casually denied his request.

Declan and Ash finished their lunches, and the day progressed like so many others. I took Hank's plate of two grapes, put it back in the refrigerator, and unbuckled him from his seat.

"Hank, remember you have to eat these grapes before you eat *anything* at dinner time," I warned. "And you're not getting a snack either."

"I don't like grapes," he said defiantly.

Dinner time rolled around at five o'clock, and I have to believe it became clear to Hank that I had taken the gloves off. When the doorbell rang, I let Hank run to the door to see the nice man holding the horizontal, flat, heat-insulated bag that even a three-year-old could recognize. I opened the door and paid the man as the smell of cheese pizza from Hank's favorite pizza delivery wafted in with me.

We sat down for dinner. I served the rest of us pizza and carrots, and Hank got his plate of two grapes.

He offered to eat the carrots instead. This time, I thought I detected a hint of desperation.

Request denied.

Declan started in on him, "Hank, grapes are good. Why don't you just eat them?"

"Because I don't like grapes," he said, looking back and forth several times between Declan's pizza and his grapes like he was watching a ping pong rally.

Maybe it was out of respect for his iron will or worry that I was taking this a little far with a three-year-old, but I conceded a bit and told him I would make him anything he wanted for dinner if he ate the grapes.

"Seriously, Hank, anything! Chicken-dinos. Grilled cheese. Chocolate chip pancakes. Pizza. Whatever you want. But you have to eat both of those grapes."

He sat through dinner, pushed the grapes around the plate a bit, but he held fast to his refusal as I cleared the rest of dinner away and started the dishes. I put his grapes back in the fridge with a last, calm but stern warning, "You will not eat breakfast tomorrow until you eat these grapes." I let him out of his booster, and the evening progressed uneventfully.

Until 7:30 p.m. He broke at 7:30 p.m.

He approached me and declared he was willing to eat the grapes if he could have dinner. Concealing both my relief and my satisfaction, I sat him in his booster and put the grapes on the plastic plate down in front of him. He made one last-second plea for mercy, "Can I just eat one of them?" He asked.

"Nope. You have to eat both." I had him against the ropes; it was checkmate, and I was not about to be manipulated.

He stared at the grapes for a bit and then picked one up and took one of those tiny bites that barely scrapes the skin off the outside of the grape.

"It's going to take you a long time to eat those if you take bites that small," I told him.

He put the grape in, chewed, and swallowed. His expression, blank at first, changed to mild surprise as if he thought the grapes were going to hurt in some way that never materialized. I said, "See, they're pretty good, don't you think?"

He shrugged and said, "They're okay," before eating the second grape. "Can I have pizza and dino-chicken now?"

"Yes, you can," I said with relief.

He ate his dinner ravenously and went to bed happy. I also went to bed happy, savoring my victory over such a strong competitor.

The next morning, I could have been magnanimous. I could have let the waters cool a bit before enforcing this new policy to which I had now committed us. But that is not how one wins this type of battle. I needed to hammer the point home. Thus, I made a great breakfast. Homemade French toast with whipped cream and bacon on the side. Another of Hank's favorite combinations.

Hank got a plate with three grapes on it this time. "Gotta eat the grapes first, buddy."

He stared at the grapes with the 33% increase and then pushed his plate ever so slightly away. I couldn't believe it. The kid actually skipped breakfast, and the Standoff began again. I shouldn't have been surprised. Just a couple of months earlier, when we were potty-training him, Hank told me he planned to ask Santa Claus for a skateboard. I was a little concerned about a three-year-old having a skateboard, so I let him know that Santa would not even consider bringing him a skateboard unless Hank pooped in the toilet. I figured it was worth it for him to get a skateboard from Santa if I could wrap up the whole potty-training nightmare in one package.

"I don't want a skateboard," he said without hesitation or remorse. And that was that. He just thought of other toys to ask Santa to bring. This is what I was dealing with.

So when lunchtime came at noon on the second day of the Standoff, I served Hank his plate of three grapes and made his favorite soup, Italian Wedding Soup, for Declan and Ash. There was no need for threats or cajoling because everyone knew the rules by this time. Hank decided to skip lunch, too, and the grapes went back into the fridge. I worried I was in for a more resolved hunger strike, but fortunately, my fear was misplaced. At 2:30 p.m., he broke and agreed to eat the grapes. This time, he ate all three without hesitation or fanfare. And this time, he seemed to like them. I let up on him for dinner that night and made a dish that he actually liked with a vegetable that he was accustomed to eating: broccoli. Go figure.

The next morning, Hank tried cantaloupe for the first time. No threats or bribes necessary. After that, he could still be a little picky from time to time, but since losing the Standoff, he would try anything I put on a plate.

Cue the music. Don't mess with Clint.

TEACHER APPRECIATION WEEK

Each year, "Teacher Appreciation Week" occurs in our schools, at every grade level, for every teacher. It sounds nice but it is basically a mom's competition to show who appreciates their kid's teachers the most. In our community, its disruptiveness is eclipsed only by its absurdity.

The email onslaught usually begins about a month prior. If "Reply All" were a button, I would have ripped it off the keyboard years ago. What is it with women and Reply All? Yes, sometimes it can be necessary and helpful in event planning, but that does not mean everyone needs to know that you can't come and won't be bringing anything. Just tell the planner and spare the rest of us!

Anyway, by the time The Week actually rolls around, I'm so sick of hearing about this week's requirements that I make a yearly vow for us to be on vacation the next year. This year was no different. Thank God for the parents willing to harass the rest of us nonresponsive ingrates, but really, do we have to provide flowers for every teacher? Why do we assume teachers are so short on flowers? We write cards, give gifts, attend coffee socials, and bring flowers. Always flowers.

With three young kids, one of whom attends two pre-K schools, The Week feels like the week before a family wedding with all the requirements. This time, I painstakingly marked my calendar with each day's respective duties. I specifically wrote "Ash brings flowers" on the days where—you guessed it—Ash was supposed to bring flowers. One would think I was adequately prepared. But when flower day came, I quickly realized I had forgotten something as I dropped her off at school. Kids were arriving with floral bouquets. Some had obviously visited the local florist and spent big money. Others hand-picked beautiful arrangements from their gardens. Ash had nothing but her *Dora the Explorer* lunch bag.

I was not going to go to the store (or the florist!) at this point, so I considered my remaining options. Spring had not sprung enough to produce even a stand of Dandelions outside to poach. Probably for the better since a handful of scrubby

Dandelions might have been the one gesture more insulting than forgetting flowers entirely. Oh well, screw flower day.

Fortunately, two days later, I redeemed myself. Just prior to loading Ash into the minivan to rush to school, I remembered it was "make-a-card" day. Finally, those scraps of construction paper would be put to good use! Ashleigh selected the proper color, and I took the time to draw a flower (the irony only hitting me as I write now) on the cover of the card. One card seemed sufficient to thank three teachers, and I was pretty sure I couldn't duplicate another perfectly sketched daisy, so off we went for school.

It was a smashing success. Remember, the competition is between moms, so the bar for dads is low on these things. A stay-at-home mom would have made three cards, but since I had succeeded in lowering expectations even further by forgetting flowers, I pretty much owned make-a-card day.

When the week drew to a close, I took stock of my Teacher Appreciation Week performance: Donated to class gift—check. Cards for all teachers—check. RSVP to the teacher's thank you ice cream social—check. So what if I erred on flower day? Screw flower day.

With all my success during my sixth year of Teacher Appreciation Week, it is understandable how I could have missed the written reminder regarding Ashleigh's birthday celebration scheduled for the following week. Right? Her teacher scheduled her birthday celebration on her actual birthday, so there was no chance I'd forget that. By the way, if

I had known Ashleigh's birthday was going to annually follow these teacher appreciation weeks, I might have attempted to delay that pregnancy by a month or two.

Ashleigh's preschool had a birthday tradition I had forgotten from the older kids. A little prior to the kid's birthday, the class chalks a line around the birthday-kid's body onto paper. Then, they cut out the life-sized outline for the family to decorate and bring to school on the day planned to celebrate the kid's birthday. One would think that since this is my third child to attend this two-year preschool, I would have remembered this drill. One would have been wrong to think that.

So, as Teacher Appreciation Week concluded and Ashleigh's teacher handed me the rolled up, life-sized, "birthday body" and reminded me of the in-class celebration, I think I may not have been paying close attention. In my mind, I had her birthday planned. Loretta and I were just going to throw some doughnut holes at the class on the morning of her birthday as we dropped Ashleigh off, and that would be that. On the heels of Teacher Appreciation Week, that is all I could handle.

A week later, the big morning came; Loretta and I drove separate cars because she had meetings in Seattle immediately following. Loretta and Ashleigh were happy because Ashleigh got the semi-rare opportunity to ride to school in Mommy's car. In the back of my mind, I wondered why Loretta was coming to this but assumed she was trying to make the doughnut delivery more special for Ash. Either that or she was capitalizing on an opportunity to arrive late to work.

I stopped at the grocery store for the doughnut holes on the way as Loretta drove Ashleigh to school in Loretta's car. When I arrived in Ashleigh's class with the plastic grocery store bag of birthday doughnut holes, Ashleigh ran up to me and asked, "Where's my birthday body?"

You know how you stare, frozen, when someone asks you something and all the eyes in the room turn your way? Well, that is what happened right then. A slight panic set in. I realized Loretta was here because she understood there was more going on this morning than a doughnut hole drop. She looked at me with that, *Oh my God, what did you forget to do?* look. Then it hit me. I knew *exactly* where that birthday body was.

I knew it was precisely where I put it after receiving it a week ago: parked right outside, still in my minivan. "Of course, I have your birthday body, Ash!" In truth, I almost tossed it about ten times during the previous week. I was sick of seeing the rolled poster wedged between the passenger seat and center console, extending into the foot area. Now, here I was, about to be the hero and avoid the "Oh my God, what did you forget to do?" comment that was about to accompany the look of the same name.

As I was jogging confidently out to my car to get the birthday body, it occurred to me that the reason I was getting it was because they were going to put it up on the wall, and somewhere in the back of my mind, I started to worry: *Oh my God, I think I forgot to do something.*

I brought the rolled-up paper body outline into class and helped Ash take the rubber bands off. As it unfurled, the following note gently floated to the ground like a leaf:

> *"This is your child's **Birthday Body.** [Note: it was bolded in the original] Please take it home and help your child decorate it for their in-school birthday celebration. Bring it back the day we celebrate their birthday. They can use anything they want to decorate it; photos of themselves or things they like to do, drawings, they can paint it, glue fabric or sparkles to it ... there are no limits! We will send it back home with you at the end of the week. Thank you!"*

Whoops. Apparently, there are *some* limits.

As we unrolled it fully, we revealed its neglected, undecorated status. No photos. No paint. No fabric or sparkles. Just a life-sized outline of Ashleigh, barren as a blank canvas. Time to improvise. We requested supplies, and Ashleigh helped us decorate it on the spot. We used crayons and pens to draw flowers (naturally) all over and filled it up with little stickers. Ashleigh had a wonderful time and never even asked why we brought grocery store doughnut holes instead of the homemade cupcakes, pies, or cookies that are typically seen at these celebrations when moms are in charge.

Tragedy narrowly averted once again. A mom would have been racked with guilt (Loretta was, and it wasn't even her fault). I walked out of class feeling like I just hit a buzzer-beating, half-court shot to win the game.

JESUS, MARY, AND JOSEPH!

Kids say the darndest things. And, on occasion, the damndest.

This afternoon, the kids were playing in the playroom, and I was preparing dinner. The door was open between the playroom and the kitchen, which allowed me to monitor the peace quotient between Declan and Hank and occasionally keep an eye on Ashleigh.

Our playroom, like many, was filled with junky toys, stuffed animals, and games. Ours is a little different, however, in that I had recently installed two rope swings. It's turning out to be the best hundred dollars I've ever spent. I went to the rig shop at the West Marine store and had them splice two thick lines with a loop at each end so I could hang each line using chains latched to eye hooks bolted into the studs in our nine-foot ceiling. The ropes were for the bigger kids, and I also bought red plastic Clifford the Dog swings (that allow a kid to sit inside) for Ashleigh and her play date buddies.

An argument over who got which swing erupted between Declan and Hank. I wasn't really paying much attention until I heard Hank say, "Fuck no!"

STORIES FROM SAM

Hank is four years old.

I think I may have jumped over the kitchen island that blocked a direct path into the playroom.

"Hank! What did you just say?" I yelled.

He may be four, but he is no dummy. Immediately sensing he might have said something bad, he answered the way any kid would: "Nothing."

Loretta and I have always been pretty strict on language, and we endeavor not to break our own rules around the kids. We have a friend who will exclaim, "Jesus, Mary, and Joseph!" in an attempt to suppress her true emotive vocabulary. Since our kids are only six, four, and two, it's not exactly a big issue for us. We ask them to say "bottom" rather than "butt," "Oh my Gosh" rather than "Oh my God," and we forbid rude talk like saying "shut up." We try to follow the same edicts and obviously refrain from the fifty-cent swear words when little ears are present.

At least, that is what *I* do.

"Hank, what did you say?" I used my calm-through-gritted-teeth voice, and he could see that I meant business.

He looked down and whispered, "Fuck no."

"Where did you learn that?" I asked.

"Nowhere."

"Do you know what that means?"

"No."

BALANCE IS BULLSHIT

"Hank, where did you learn that word?"

> "WHERE DID YOU LEARN THAT WORD?" I REPEATED MENACINGLY.
>
> HE PAUSED ...
>
> "MOMMY."

The room was silent. Declan watched the drama unfold, knowing something was obviously wrong with what Hank said, but confused because she didn't know the meaning of the "F-word" either.

"Where did you learn that word?" I repeated menacingly.

He paused ..."Mommy."

It took all of the strength I could muster to suppress the smile lifting the corners of my mouth. I actually had to step out of the room for a second, compose myself, and then reenter to explain that we never say that word and what the punishment would be if it was spoken again. The kids seemed to understand but were also aware they were now privy to something powerful, grown-up, and bad. Rather than calling, I decided to wait until Loretta got home from work to have this chat. She's generally resistant to my attempts at cross-examination, but I knew I had her, so I wanted to discuss this face-to-face.

When she arrived home, I filled her in on Hank's expanded vocabulary, which he credited to her. Loretta feigned shock and initially denied he learned the word from her, but I had an eyewitness: Declan cited the exact time and place Loretta last used it, and the game was up.

Grinning, I looked at Loretta and shook my head in mock disapproval. "Well, Well, Well ...." I said in a most righteous tone. No other words were necessary.

BLOODY THURSDAY

It's better to be lucky than good. Declan turned 11 on February 11, 2012, so naturally, I was on top of scheduling her annual doctor's visit and physical. By *on top*, of course, I mean three months later in May 2012.

I picked up Declan early from school on May 10th to drive her to her 3 p.m. doctor's appointment. After the usual how-was-school chat, we settled in, listening to music on the radio as the doctor's office, only about one mile away, fast approached.

We were four blocks away when it occurred to me that this was Declan's 11-year-old appointment, and the subject of a girl's physical development might be discussed. *Shit.* As far as I knew, the subject of Declan's physical development had not been discussed at home as of yet. This was a task I had long ago assigned Loretta. I think Loretta hoped Declan would read a Judy Bloom novel and figure it out on her own because I had not heard of any talk of periods, bras, or breast-buds.

My understanding was that Loretta and Declan were going to attend a class for prepubescent girls and their moms at a local hospital, and the whole thing was going to be addressed in one long and awkward afternoon. Short of that, I also believed Loretta would be the one to explain periods and breasts since, as a guy, those topics were above my pay grade.

Knowing that Declan and Loretta were the perfect storm of not-really-interested-in-discussing-the-topic, I faced the fact that it was now left to me unless I wanted to look like a negligent parent in front of our doctor.

As we crested the top of a long hill, I took a deep breath, turned down Taylor Swift, and asked, "So, Declan, you took health this year as part of one of your science classes for school, right?"

"Yeah, I guess," she said, noncommittally.

"And you guys learned about how changes occur in your bodies as you get a little older, right?" This is called a "leading question" in court.

"Um, not really." This is not the answer the leading questioner was hoping for.

I'm starting to sweat just a bit now, but I press on, "Really? They didn't teach you about what happens with girls as they get close to being teenagers?"

"Nope."

Jesus Christ. She is not making this easy.

"Well, has Mommy discussed it with you?" Why did I even ask this question?

"Nope."

Awesome. We are now pulling into the doctor's office parking lot, fortunately, several minutes early, so I suggest we wait here for a minute before going in.

"So, have you learned about periods?"

She shook her head. "No, what is that?"

Oh boy. Still not ready to wade in all the way, I desperately start grabbing at straws, "So you've never talked about this stuff with your friends either?"

"No."

"Grace?"

"No."

"Kate?"

"No."

"Stella."

"No."

"No one?"

"No."

I am now officially out of ideas and straws toward which to grasp. It was time to jump in.

"Okay, so here's the deal. Girls and boys go through different changes as they get older. You know how you wear deodorant sometimes because you started to sweat a little more than before?"

She nods.

"Well, girls go through other changes as well, and it usually starts happening when they turn eleven or twelve or thirteen. Your body changes. For boys, their voices change. Girls start growing boobs, you know—that stuff. You really don't know what a 'period' is?"

"Nope."

Of course not.

"Okay, well, a period is something that happens to every woman every month for a couple of days. It's also called menstruation. Basically, what happens is that a little bit of blood comes out of your vagina over the course of a few days, and it's just your body getting rid of the blood. It doesn't hurt like when you cut yourself, but it's pretty uncomfortable for a lot of girls. It surprises you the first time because you're not expecting it, and all of a sudden, there's blood down there, so it can kind of freak out a girl who is not ready for it."

I'm periodically attempting eye contact either in the rearview mirror or with a quick turnaround while pretending to gather things up around me. She's having none of the eye contact and appears mesmerized by something (nothing) on her hand.

STORIES FROM SAM

"This happens to mommy, and your grandma (okay, I stretched a bit), and every other woman you know, so it's not a big deal; it's just what happens. And when it happens, women wear a pad down in their underwear that soaks up the blood, and that pad is called a tampon. (I know a pad is different from a tampon, but I was going for big-picture here.) They know when their period comes after a while because it only happens every 30 days (using "only," I hoped to make it sound infrequent). So if it came on May 15th, it would probably come the next time on June 15th. Some girls get pretty worked up about this when it starts happening, but you're pretty mellow about stuff, so I'd be surprised if it freaked you out in any way."

I continued with the most important part, "Oh yeah, and Dr. Schreuder may ask you about this during your appointment, but I can answer any other questions you have, too. Do you have any?"

"Not really."

Thank God. 2:58 p.m.—two minutes to spare.

"Okay, let's go in."

After the nurse took us back to one of the little exam rooms and assessed Declan's vitals, Dr. Schreuder knocked and entered. Dr. Schreuder is basically my age, married with kids, and he attended the same grade school as Loretta, a couple of years behind her.

"Declan, how are you?" He said, smiling enthusiastically.

"Good," she said in that slow, two-syllable way kids say it when they're not exactly convinced of its accuracy.

"Wow, I can't believe you're already eleven! Let's take a look ..."

He began the exam, and not three minutes went by before he said, "So Declan, you're eleven now. Have you guys talked about changes in your body, like menstruation or periods?"

And like a pro, she said, "Yeah, we've talked about it."

"Oh, great, well let me explain it a little more ...."

Dr. Schreuder shot me an approving look. I just shrugged like this was not my first rodeo.

t w e n t y - o n e

THE NEXT CHAPTER IS YOURS

If this book resonated with you—if it gave you clarity, confidence, or the push to start building a life that truly feels like yours—then mission accomplished. That's exactly why I wrote it.

The truth is, you don't need a perfect plan to create your dream life. You need clarity, courage, and the right support at the right time. If you're ready for your next step, I'd be honored to walk alongside you.

Creating a life that feels aligned and meaningful doesn't happen overnight, but you don't have to figure it out alone. Here are a few ways I support women like you every day:

1:1 COACHING—

Whether you're leading through complexity, launching something new, or simply trying to find your rhythm at work and at home, this is your space to reset, realign, and move forward with clarity and purpose.

We'll define success on your terms, build confidence to make bold, aligned decisions, and create a plan that actually fits your real life.

STRATEGIC CONSULTING—

From growth strategy and brand positioning to leadership alignment and strategic intensives, I bring 30+ years of experience scaling businesses, building brands, and advising at the highest levels.

THE FOUNDERS CIRCLE—

A private community for women who are building something meaningful while balancing life, love, and everything in between.

Monthly strategy sessions, expert tools, and honest conversations with a small group of ambitious women who truly get it. Because you don't have to figure it out alone.

SPEAKING & EVENTS—

From keynote stages to intimate retreats, I speak on bold leadership, sustainable success, and the truth behind "having it all." Looking for a message that's real, relatable, and rooted in experience? Let's talk.

THE CONVERSATION CONTINUES—

The same honest voice you found in these pages—now in your ears. As an unapologetic entrepreneur, I continue developing new opportunities to connect with my audience. Join me for real conversations, practical tools, and unfiltered stories designed to keep you grounded, growing, and inspired to take bold next steps.

To be the first to know when my next thing launches, sign up for my newsletter:

lorettasoffe.com

SPREAD THE WORD—

If something here helped you, share it. Your story might be the spark someone else needs.

You don't need to do it all.

You just need to do it your way.

You've got this—and I've got you.

Cheers,

Loretta

PS: This may be crazy, but feel free to email me:

loretta@lorettasoffe.com

BALANCE IS BULLSHIT

ASHLEIGH, SAM, HANK, LORETTA, DECLAN

CONNECT WITH LORETTA SOFFE

ACKNOWLEDGMENTS

Like most things in my life, this book came together through grit, grace, and the steady support of the people around me. It was a big undertaking, but most days, I felt divinely inspired, and that deep sense of purpose gave me the motivation and stamina to see it through.

I could never have done it alone—**Sam**, **Wendy**, **Declan**, **Hank**, **Ashleigh**, **Gabe**, and so many others showed up at every turn, proving that big dreams are always a team sport.

To **my parents**, whose leap of faith from Ireland to Seattle showed me what courage looks like, and to my four siblings—the original crew who cheered (and challenged) me into becoming who I am.

To **Sam's parents**, **Steve** and **Colleen**, and **Sam's sister K.C.** and **husband Brian**, thank you for embracing me as your own and modeling a partnership grounded in humor and heart.

To **my swim teammates** who pushed me, raced me, and cheered me on through predawn workouts, brutal sets, and travel meets—you made me tougher, faster, and proved the best wins (and lessons) come from doing it together.

To **my Nordstrom family**—mentors, colleagues, employees, direct reports, and Pete and Eric—your brilliance sharpened my instincts and kept the bar sky-high.

And to **the yogis** who remind me to breathe: you keep me centered and strong.

Tremendous gratitude to **my editorial dream team—Wendy and Sam**, and the **tireless Beta readers** who challenged every sentence in service of every reader. You turned messy drafts into something meaningful and beautiful.

To **my ride-or-die friends** from Mercer Island, Bellevue, Seattle, California, NYC, and Texas … all the way to London and St. Barths—decades of laughs, tears, dancing, and real talk have carried me farther than you know. Your unwavering support, near or far, has been the steady heartbeat behind so much of this. The distance, the texts, the calls, and everything in between have only made your presence feel louder, closer, and more inspiring.

And finally, **to the women (and the people who love them) who pick up this book looking for a new way forward**—you are why I wrote it.

And to **everyone who believed that Balance is Bullshit long before it was acceptable to say so**—thank you for giving me permission to speak the truth we've all been thinking.

This book is proof that life doesn't have to be perfect to be extraordinary. It just has to be real, intentional, and authentically yours.

The best is yet to come.

CHEERS,

LORETTA

NOTES

NOTES

NOTES

NOTES

NOTES

NOTES

www.ingramcontent.com/pod-product-compliance
Lightning Source LLC
Chambersburg PA
CBHW050523100526
44581CB00002B/91